THAI FOLKLORE

Table of Contents

Doi Nang Non 1
Himavanta 2
Jatukham Rammathep 2
Khun Chang Khun Phaen 3
Luang Pu Thuat 8
Nang Kwak 9
Nariphon 10
Phi Fa 11
Phi Ta Khon 11
Phraya Anuman Rajadhon 12
Phra Aphai Mani 14
Phra Mae Thorani 14
Rocket Festival 16
Ruesi 20
Sangsilchai 21
Suvannamaccha 21
Thens 22
The Twelve Sisters 22
Vessantara Jataka 25
Yantra tattooing 27

Preface

Each chapter in this book ends with a URL to a hyperlinked online version. Use the online version to access related pages, websites, footnotes, tables, color photos, updates, or to see the chapter's contributors. Click the edit link to suggest changes. Please type the URL exactly as it appears. If you change the URL's capitalization, for example, it may not work.

Purchase of this book entitles you to a free trial membership in the publisher's book club at www.booksllc.net. (Time limited offer.) Simply enter the barcode number from the back cover onto the membership form on our home page. The book club entitles you to select from millions of books at no additional charge, including a PDF copy of this and related books to read on the go. Simply enter the title or subject onto the search form to find them.

If you have any questions, could you please be so kind as to consult our Frequently Asked Questions page at www.booksllc.net/faqs.cfm? You are also welcome to contact us there.

Publisher: Books LLC, Wiki Series, Memphis, TN, USA, 2013.

Doi Nang Non

Doi Nang Non

Elevation	830 m (2,723 ft)
Listing	List of mountain ranges in the world named The Sleeping Lady
Location	
Chiang Rai (Thailand)	
Range	Daen Lao Range
Coordinates	20°21′06″N 99°50′30″E
Geology	
Type	karstic
Climbing	
Easiest route	drive

Doi Nang Non (Thai: ดอยนางนอน), "Mountain of the Sleeping Lady", is an unusual land feature of the Thai highlands located in Chiang Rai Province, Thailand. It is a karstic formation part of the southern end of the Daen Lao Range with numerous waterfalls and caves.

Location

Doi Nang Non consists of a long hill tract that lies on the western side of the highway between Chiang Rai and Mae Sai. The greater part of the range is in Mae Chan District, extending west and south west of Pong Pha. The silhouette of the mountain range takes the shape of a reclining woman with long hair when seen from certain angles.

Legend

The main legend of Thai folklore on how this land feature came into being says that there was once a beautiful young princess in the area whose lover left her pregnant and went away. He gave her a ring and promised he would come back. The lady became anxious and waited, but time passed and her lover wouldn't come. Suddenly the woman thought that her husband might be lost and went out of the house to search for him. She wandered anxiously for days through fields and forests all across the region, but couldn't find him. However, the lady didn't give up and walked and walked until she could walk no more.

Then she realized that her lover had abandoned her and took of her engagement ring and threw it far away, so that it landed at Nong Waen (หนองแหวน) in Mae Chan Subdistrict. At that point the young lady was so exhausted she fell down on her back with her head towards Doi Tung and her feet pointing at Doi Mae Salong. Looking at the sky she cried bitterly, finally dying of despair and a broken heart. After her death the woman's ghost grew to a huge size and was covered by the surrounding earth, taking the shape of a sleeping lady (Nang Non; นางนอน) with her face looking skywards. Her belly with her unborn baby inside became separated from her body and was turned into the nearby mountain of Doi Tung.

Tourism

There is a viewpoint at Amphoe Mae Chan, Mae Chan District, from where the "sleeping lady" can be observed best. Local tour guides like to joke that Doi Nang Non is "the highest mountain in the world", if the lady would get up and stand on her feet.

There are a number of caves and water courses in these hills. Some of them have been developed as a tourist attraction.

Tum Luang is a cave inside the Doi Nang Non mountain massif with numerous stalactites and stalagmites. It is a very long cave with branches that go on for several kilometres.

Khun Naam Naang Non is a natural pond into which water flows from the rocks above. This water is said to be the tears of the lady's ghost.

Source http://en.wikipedia.org/wiki/Doi_Nang_Non

Himavanta

Thai lacquerwork painting of the Nariphon tree at Phra Pathom Chedi

The **Himmavanta** (Thai: ป่าหิมพานต์}, *Pa Himaphan*) is a legendary forest which surrounds the base of Mount Meru in Hindu mythology. It is said to be the home of an assortment of mythical creatures, such as the *naga*, the *kinnara* and the *garuda*.

The mythical Nariphon tree of Buddhist mythology, often mentioned in Thai folklore, is said to grow there.

List of animals of Himavanta

Source http://en.wikipedia.org/wiki/Himavanta

Jatukham Rammathep

Jatukham Rammathep is the name of an unusually popular amulet sold by some Buddhist temples in Thailand. The amulet is named for two princes of the Srivijaya kingdom of southern Thailand, and is believed to provide protection and good fortune to the bearer. Some legends hold that the name actually belongs to an incarnation of the Bodhisattva Avalokitesvara, whose worship was known in the south due to the presence of Mahayana Buddhism there during earlier eras.

The original Jatukham Rammathep amulets were created in 1987 by a Thai policeman named Khun Phantharak Rajjadej who believed that the spirit of Jatukham Rammathep had assisted him in solving a difficult murder case.

During 2006, following on the death of Khun Phantharak Rajjadej, Jatukham Rammathep amulets began to grow wildly in popularity among Thais who believed in their ability to grant good fortune and solve personal problems. The amulets were initially distributed by a temple in the town of Nakhon Si Thammarat in southern Thailand. As the demand for these amulets grew, they began to also be produced at other temples in Thailand.

In April 2007, a woman died after being trampled in a rush to acquire reservations for a batch of Jatukham Rammathep amulets being produced at the Mahathat Woromaha Vihan temple in Nakhon Si Thammarat. Later that month, in the face of a crime wave of daily amulet robberies, Thailand's Supreme Patriarch stopped providing materials from the temple, such as ash from incense, used to make the amulets.

Trucks with loudspeakers blare promotions for different series of amulets all day in Nakhon Si Thammarat, and colorful posters cover many walls.

It is estimated that sales of the Jatukham Rammathep amulet in Thailand will amount to over 20 billion baht during 2007.

Source http://en.wikipedia.org/wiki/Jatukham_Rammathep

Khun Chang Khun Phaen

Khun Phaen and Wanthong flee to the forest. Mural from sala on Khao Phra, U Thong.

Nang Phim, Wat Pa Lelai, Suphanburi, Thailand

Khun Chang Khun Phaen (Thai: ขุนช้างขุนแผน) is an epic Thai poem which originated from a legend of Thai folklore and is one of the most notable works in Thai literature. Chang and Phaen are the leading male characters, and "Khun" was a junior feudal title given for male commoners. The story is a classic love triangle, ending in high tragedy. Khun Phaen (dashing but poor) and Khun Chang (rich but ugly) compete for the lovely Wanthong from childhood for over fifty years. Their contest involves two wars, several abductions, a suspected revolt, an idyllic sojourn in the forest, two court cases, trial by ordeal, jail, and treachery. Ultimately the king condemns Wanthong to death for failing to choose between the two men. The poem was written down in the early nineteenth century, and a standard printed edition first published in 1917–1918. Like many works with origins in popular entertainment, it is fast-moving and stuffed full of heroism, romance, sex, violence, rude-mechanical comedy, magic, horror, and passages of lyrical beauty. In Thailand, the story is universally known. Children learn passages at school, and the poem is a source of songs, popular sayings, and everyday metaphors.

Origins and *sepha*

Modern performance of *sepha*, showing *krap*.

Khun Chang Khun Phaen is an old story in the Thai language. It originated as a folktale some time before the eighteenth century, developed by storytellers who recited episodes for local audiences, and passed on the story by word-of-mouth. By the eighteenth century, such performances had become the most popular form of entertainment in Siam. The storytellers recounted the story in stylized recitation, using two small sticks of wood (*krap*) to give rhythm and emphasis. The performances typically lasted a full night.

The performance of *Khun Chang Khun Phaen* created a new genre known as *sepha*. For at least a century, only episodes from this work were known by this term. In the Fourth Reign (1851–1868), parts of the royal chronicles and a few other works were also rendered in this form on royal commission, but all but a few fragments have since disappeared.

The origin of this word *sepha* is disputed. There is a musical form of the same name, but this seems unconnected. Kukrit Pramoj thought that sepha meant a jail and that the genre was developed by convicts in jail. Sujit Wongthet argued a connection to the Sanskrit word *sewa*, indicating some original association with ritual.

Khun Chang and Khun Phaen are the names of the two leading male characters. In the era when the poem's events are set, Khun was a title for one of the lowest ranks in the official nobility.

Development as literature

Beginning in the eighteenth century, prominent episodes from the story were written down. After the foundation of Bangkok in 1782, the new royal court made efforts to retrieve all kinds of texts which had survived the sack of Ayutthaya fifteen years earlier. Episodes of *Khun Chang Khun Phaen* were transcribed from earlier texts, or adapted from recitations by storytellers. No manuscripts of *Khun Chang Khun Phaen* have survived from the Ayutthaya era.

It became conventional to render these written versions in the then-popular poetic meter, *klon*, especially the variant with eight-syllable lines known as *klon paet*. Performance of these episodes were popular in the court and among the aristocracy. In the Second Reign (1809–1824), the performance was often enhanced by adding music. From the Fourth Reign (1851–1868), dancing was also added and more than one performer might share the task of recitation.

Several chapters were written down by members of the literary salon of King Rama II (1809–1824). None of these works are signed, but certain chapters and part-chapters are conventionally attributed to King Rama II, the future King Rama III (r. 1824–1851), and the great poet Sunthorn Phu. Another member of the salon, Prince Mahasak Phonlasep, a son of King Rama I (1782–1809) and cousin of King Rama II, may also have contributed to the writing.

Several other chapters were compiled later, probably during the reign of King Rama III, by Khru Jaeng, a performer of *sepha* and other forms of entertainment. Little is known of him except for an internal reference in the poem. For over half the 43 chapters in the standard version, the author is unknown.

A former missionary, Samuel Smith, printed the first book version in 1872, probably using a manuscript belonging to Somdet Chaophraya Borommaha Sisuriyawong. Another printed version was issued in 1889 by the Wat Ko Press. Five episodes composed by Khru Jaeng were printed around 1890.

The standard modern edition appeared in three volumes in 1917–1918, published by the Wachirayan Library, and edited by its head, Prince Damrong Rachanubhab. Damrong compiled from four sets of *samut thai* manuscripts and a few other fragments. The earliest of the manuscripts dated from the Fourth Reign (1851–1868). He selected what he believed were the best versions of each episode, and added some link passages. He deleted some passages which he considered obscene, and some which depended on topical jokes and other material which he felt were no longer comprehensible.

This standard edition is around 20,000 lines divided into 43 chapters. The main story ends in chapter 36, but a further seven chapters were included because the episodes were well-known and popular. Performers and authors had already developed many more episodes which extended the story down through three generations of Khun Phaen's lineage. Damrong decreed that these were not good enough as either narrative or poetry to deserve publication. Around fifty of these later chapters have since been published in various collections.

Plot

Khun Chang, Phlai Kaeo (who later is

Model of Khun Chang's house at Wat Palelai, Suphanburi.

Old Thai house erected on site of Ayutthaya jail, and called Khun Phaen's House.

given the title, Khun Phaen), and Nang Phim Philalai (who later changes her name to Wanthong) are childhood friends in Suphanburi. Khun Phaen is handsome and intelligent, but poor because the king has executed his father and seized their property. He enters the monkhood as a novice to get educated, excelling at military skills and love magic. Khun Chang is ugly and stupid, but rich and well-connected at the Ayutthaya court.

By age 15, Phim is the belle of Suphanburi. She meets Phlai Kaeo when putting food in his almsbowl at Songkran (Thai New Year). Sparks fly. They have a passionate affair, with him shuttling between the wat (Buddhist monastery) and her bedroom.

Khun Chang is also smitten by Phim. He competes for her using his wealth and status. He offers to give her mother Phim's weight in gold. After Phlai Kaeo and Phim are married, Khun Chang maneuvers the king to send Phlai Kaeo on military service, and then claims he is dead. When Phlai Kaeo returns victorious, Khun Chang plots to have him banished from Ayutthaya for negligence on government service.

Phim (now Wanthong) resists Khun Chang. But when Phlai Kaeo (now Khun Phaen) returns from war with another wife, they have a jealous quarrel. Wanthong goes to live with Khun Chang, enjoying his devotion and the comforts afforded by his wealth.

When Khun Phaen's second wife, Laothong, is taken into the palace by the king, Khun Phaen regrets abandoning Wanthong. He breaks into Khun Chang's house at the dead of night and takes Wanthong away. At first she is reluctant to leave her comfortable existence, but the passion rekindles, and they flee to an idyllic but frugal sojourn in the forest.

Khun Chang tells the king that Khun Phaen is mounting a rebellion. The king sends an army which Khun Phaen defeats, killing two of its officers. A warrant is issued for his arrest. When Wanthong becomes pregnant, Khun Phaen decides to leave the forest and give himself up. At the trial, the charges of rebellion are disproved, and Khun Chang is heavily fined.

Khun Phaen angers the king by asking for the release of Laothong. He is jailed, and festers in prison for around twelve years. Khun Chang abducts Wanthong and they again live together in Suphanburi.

Wanthong gives birth to Phlai Ngam, her son with Khun Phaen. When Phlai Ngam is eight, Khun Chang tries to kill him. Phlai Ngam escapes to live in Kanchanaburi with his grandmother who teaches him from Khun Phaen's library.

When the kings of Ayutthaya and Chiang Mai quarrel over a beautiful daughter of the King of Vientiane, Phlai Ngam volunteers to lead an army to Chiang Mai, and successfully petitions for Khun Phaen's release. They capture the King of Chiang Mai, and return with the Vientiane princess and a great haul of booty. Khun Phaen now gains status as the governor of Kanchanaburi. Phlai Ngam is appointed Phra Wai, an officer in the royal pages.

Khun Chang gets drunk at Phra Wai's wedding, and the old rivalry returns. Phra Wai abducts Wanthong from Khun Chang's house, prompting Khun Chang to petition the king for redress. At the subsequent trial, the king demands that Wanthong decide between Khun Chang and Khun Phaen. She cannot, and is dumb-struck. The king orders her execution. Phra Wai pleads successfully with the king for a reprieve, but the order arrives fractionally too late to avoid her execution.

Origins of the story

Prince Damrong believed that the *Khun Chang Khun Phaen* story was based on true events which took place around 1500 in the reign of King Ramathibodi II. His evidence was a memoir believed to have been taken down from Thai prisoners in Burma after the fall of Ayutthaya in 1767 (*Khamhaikan chao krung kao*, The testimony of the inhabitants of the old capital). The memoir mentions the name of Khun Phaen in an account of a military campaign against Chiang Mai. However, this memoir is just as much a text of oral history as *Khun Chang Khun Phaen* itself, and could well have developed from the folktale, rather than vice versa. The campaign against Chiang Mai in the latter part of *Khun Chang Khun Phaen* seems to be modeled on events which appear in the Ayutthaya and Lanchang chronicles for the 1560s.

The opening chapter of *Khun Chang Khun Phaen* mentions a gift from the Emperor of China which might be dated shortly before 1600. The third chapter has a date based on a 120-year calendar which can be resolved as 1549/50, 1669/70, or 1789/90.

Most likely *Khun Chang Khun Phaen* developed over decades or centuries by storytellers absorbing and embellishing several local tales and true stories. Prince Damrong surmised that the original version was much shorter and simpler: Khun Phaen woos and marries Wanthong but then goes to war; Khun Chang seizes her; Khun Phaen returns and in the ensuing squabble, Wanthong is condemned to death. The story then expanded as other episodes were assembled around these leading characters. The whole second half of the standard version shows signs of being an extension which repeats themes and episodes from the first half. Certain episodes are known to have been newly written and incorporated in the nineteenth century. Some episodes are known to be modeled on true events. The arrival of an embassy from Lanchang, for example, is based on the reception of an embassy from Tavoy at Ayutthaya in 1791.

Characteristics

Realism

Most major works of old Thai literature are about gods and royalty, and take place in the court or the heavens. *Khun Chang Khun Phaen* is the great exception. The major characters are drawn from the minor provincial gentry. The authors build an atmosphere of realism by cramming the narrative with anthropological detail on dress, marriages, funerals, temple ceremonies, feasts (including menus and recipes), court cases, trial by ordeal, house building, travel, and entertainment.

In addition, the geography is real. Most of the action takes place in Suphanburi, Kanchanaburi, and Ayutthaya, and the locations are easily identifiable today, including temples and cross-country routes. Several places mentioned in the text appear on some early nineteenth century maps which were recently discovered in the royal palace in Bangkok.

In the later part of the tale there is an expedition to Vientiane which clearly follows one of the routes taken by Bangkok armies during the war against Vientiane in 1827–1828. There are also two military campaigns to Chiang Mai, but here the geography is much less certain. The place names are correct, but temples are located in the wrong town, routes between places make no geographical sense, and other mistakes indicate that the authors had only a hazy idea of the northern region.

Super-realism

Khun Phaen amulet.

As a novice, Phlai Kaeo is schooled in the "inner ways" (Thai: ทางใน, *thang nai*). This phrase refers to beliefs in supernatural powers which exist within human beings and other natural objects, and which can be activated through taught skills. These beliefs stem from the esoteric school of Buddhism, and are found as a substratum in Buddhism throughout Southeast Asia and other parts of the Buddhist world.

The methods to activate these latent powers include meditation and recitation of mantras or formulas (elsewhere, yoga is another method). The power can also be transferred to objects, especially diagrams known as yantra (Thai: เลขยันต์, *lek yan*). In India, where they probably originated, such diagrams are composed mostly of geometric shapes with symbolic meanings arranged in symmetrical patterns (the mandala is a yantra). In the Thai tradition, these diagrams also include numbers in sequences with supernatural meaning, pictures of gods and powerful animals (lion, tiger, elephant), and formulas or abbreviated formulas written in Pali or Khmer. To have power, these diagrams have to be drawn by an adept under strict rules (such as reciting formulas continuously, completing the drawing in one sitting), and activated by reciting a formula.

Yantra (called *yan* in Thai) diagrams can be carried on the body in various ways: tattooed on the skin (*sak yan* - สักยันต์); imprinted on a shirt or inner shirt; imprinted on a scarf (Thai: ประเจียด, *prajiat*) tied round the head, arm, or chest; imprinted on a belt, perhaps made from human skin; imprinted on paper or cloth which is then rolled and plaited into a ring (Thai: แหวนพิรอด, *waen phirot*); inscribed on a soft metal such as tin which is coiled round a cord and worn as an amulet (Thai: ตะกรุด, takrut. The main purpose of these various forms of *yan* designs with Khom inscriptions, is to give invulnerability or protection against various forms of threat.

The same purpose is served by carrying amulets made from natural materials which have some unusual property which seems contrary to nature. A good example is mercury – a metal which has the unusual property of behaving like a fluid. Other examples include cat's eye, a semi-precious stone which resembles an animal's eye, and "fluid metal" (Thai: เหล็กไหล, *lek lai*), a metal-like substance believed to become malleable under the heat of a candle's flame. These items can be strung on cords and worn around various parts of the body, or inserted under the skin.

Before going into battle or any other undertaking entailing risk, Khun Phaen decks himself with several of these items. He also consults various oracles which indicate whether the time and the direction of travel is auspicious. These oracles include casting various forms of horoscope, looking for shapes in the clouds, and examining which nostril the breath is passing most easily.

Khun Phaen is also schooled in mantras or formulas with supernatural power. They are used for such purposes as stunning enemies, transforming his body into other forms, opening locks and chains, putting everyone else to sleep, and converting sheaves of grass into invulnerable spirit warriors. Khun Phaen also uses love formulas to captivate women, and to allay the wrath of the king.

Finally, Khun Phaen has a corps of spirits which he looks after. They defend him against enemy spirits, act as spies, and transport him at speed. In a famous passage, Khun Phaen acquires an especially powerful spirit from the still-born foetus of his own son. This spirit is known as a *Gumarn Tong* (Thai: กุมารทอง), a golden child.

In the poem, the command of these powers is described using several combinations of the following words: *wicha* (Thai: วิชา), taught knowledge; *witthaya* (Thai: วิทยา), similar to the suffix, -ology; *wet* (Thai: เวท), from veda, the Brahminical scriptures; *mon* (Thai: มนตร์), mantra, a Buddhist prayer; *katha* (Thai: คาถา), a verse or formula; and *akhom* (Thai: อาคม), from *agama*, a Sanskrit word meaning knowledge, especially pre-vedic texts. These words position the command of these powers as an ancient and sacred form of learning.

Adaptations

While the poetic sepha has become the standard version of *Khun Chang Khun Phaen*, the story has been rendered into many other forms.

In the nineteenth century, various episodes were adapted into drama plays (*lakhon*), dance dramas, comedies, and *likay*. In the twentieth century, episodes were adapted into the poetical form of *nirat*, and the folk performance of *phleng choi*.

There have been five film versions, beginning with a silent film in two parts by Bamrung Naewphanit in 1936. The most recent film version, *Khun Phaen*, was directed by Thanit Jitnukul in 2002.

A first TV version appeared as a single episode in 1955. A 1970 version, based around the exploits of Khun Phaen as governor of Kanchanaburi, extended over 500 episodes. Thai Channel 3 aired a serial version under the name *Phim Phlilalai* (Wanthong's natal name) in 1985, and Thai Channel 5 aired a serial *Khun Phaen* in 1998.

A cartoon version, drawn by Sawat Jukarop, appeared in *Siam Rath* from 1932 to 1950. The latest among many book-length cartoon versions was compiled by Sukrit Boonthong in 2005.

Several famous artists have illustrated scenes from *Khun Chang Phaen*, especially Hem Vejakorn. In 1917, BAT Co Ltd issues a series of 100 cigarette cards featuring characters from the story.

There have been several adaptations into novels, beginning with Malai Chuphinit, *Chai Chatri* (The Hero) in 1932. The most famous is *Khun Phaen* written by the major thriller author Por Intharapalit in 1972.

There have been at least seven retellings of the story in modern Thai prose. The first, and most complete of these, was by Premseri in 1964.

Three other works tell the story with the addition of annotations and explanations of old words and forgotten customs. The study by Suphon Bunnag was published in two volumes in 1960, and republished in her cremation volume in 1975. Khun Wichitmatra (Sanga Kanchanakphan) and Phleuang na Nakhon wrote a series of articles in the magazine *Withayasan* over 1954–57, collected together in book form in 1961. Kukrit Pramoj also wrote a series of articles in *Siam Rath*, collected as a book in 1989.

In 2002 Sujit Wongthet published a similar work which originated as a series of articles in the magazine *Sinlapa Watthanatham* (Art and Culture). The book includes a copy of two manuscript versions of chapter 17, which Sujit secured from the National Archives under the Freedom of Information Act. These manuscripts reveal what Prince Damrong had excised in his editing.

Cholthira Satyawadhna wrote an MA dissertation in 1970 using a Freudian approach to analyze aggression in *Khun Chang Khun Phaen*. The thesis became famous, both as a landmark in Thai literary criticism, and as an early Thai feminist treatise.

In modern life

Shrine to Khun Phaen and his father Khun Krai, including a golden fighting cock, at Cockfight Hill, Kanchanaburi.

Shrine to Nang Simala at Old Phichit.

Khun Chang Khun Phaen is the source of many sayings in modern Thai, and several songs. The name Khun Phaen is shorthand for a great lover (similar to Romeo or Casanova). It is also the name of a famous amulet, reputed to bring success in love, and the slang for a large "chopper" motorcycle.

In Suphanburi and Phichit, towns which figure prominently in the poem, the major streets have been named after characters in the story.

At several locations featured in the story there are now shrines with images of the characters. Such locations include Cockfight Hill in old Kanchanaburi (images of Khun Phaen and his father

Shrine to Nang Buakhli on stalactite in cave at Ban Tham, Kanchanaburi.

Khun Krai), the old town of Phichit (Nang Simala), and Ban Tham in Kanchanaburi (Nang Buakhli).

In Ayutthaya, an old Thai house has been erected on the site of the jail where Khun Phaen was incarcerated in the poem. The house has been renamed "Khum Khun Phaen" and is a major tourist attraction. A similar house, attributed to Khun Phaen, has recently been erected in Wat Khae in Suphanburi. This temple also has an old tamarind tree which is legendarily associated with a passage in the poem in which Khun Phaen is taught how to transform tamarind leaves into wasps.

Wat Palelai, Suphanburi, has erected a model of Khun Chang's house, and commissioned a series of murals from the *Khun Chang Khun Phaen* story around its main cloister.

Contemporary status

Almost every Thai knows the story of *Khun Chang Khun Phaen*. Most children have to memorize and recite extracts at school.

Thailand's literary establishment has been rather cool towards *Khun Chang Khun Phaen*, probably because of the work's origins in the folk tradition and consequent lack of refinement. In addition, feminists have criticized the story for celebrating Khun Phaen as a promiscuous lover, and making Wanthong a tragic victim.

Kukrit Pramoj opened his study of the poem with the remark: "At present there are some knowledgeable people who have expressed the opinion that *Khun Chang Khun Phaen* is an immoral book and a bad example which should be burnt or destroyed, so no one may read it from now on."

Kukrit Pramoj is one among many enthusiasts who value *Khun Chang Khun Phaen* as a great story and as a unique repository of old Thai culture. Other prominent defenders include:

Sulak Sivaraksa (social commentator, activist): "This immortal story is number one in Thai literature, and cedes nothing to the major literary works of other nations."

Rong Wongsawan (novelist, essayist): "I like *Khun Chang Khun Phaen* and still read it today. It's the literary work which best reflects the life of the Thai. In simple words, the voice of the people."

Naowarat Phongphaibun (national poet): "Every Thai person over 30 should read at least four or five books, starting with *Khun Chang Khun Phaen*."

William J. Gedney (linguist): "I have often thought that if all other information on traditional Thai culture were to be lost, the whole complex could be reconstructed from this marvellous text."

Translation

In 2010 the first complete translation into English has been done. Before that there was no full translation into any European language. Prem Chaya (Prince Prem Purachatra) began a précis version, *The Story of Khun Chang Khun Phaen* (1955, 1959), but completed only two of the three planned volumes. J. Kasem Sibunruang compiled an abridged version in French, with some commentary, as *La femme, le heros et le vilain. Poeme populaire thai. Khun*

Chang, Khun Phen (1960). Klaus Wenk translated the famous chapter 24 by Sunthorn Phu word-for-word into German, in *Studien zur Literatur der Thai: Texte und Interpretationen von und zu Sunthon Phu und seinem Kreis*. Hamburg and Bangkok (1985).

There are very few studies on *Khun Chang Khun Phaen* in western languages. Prince Bidyalankarana (Krommuen Pitthayalongkon) wrote two articles on the poem in the *Journal of Siam Society* in 1926 and 1941 which explain the metrical form of the *sepha* and give a summary of the plot. E. H. S. Simmonds published an aritlce in *Asia Major* in 1963 which compares one episode in the standard text with a version he recorded in performance.

Khun Chang Khun Phaen has been completely translated into English by husband-and-wife team Chris Baker and Pasuk Phongpaichit in 2010.

Source http://en.wikipedia.org/wiki/Khun_Chang_Khun_Phaen

Luang Pu Thuat

The biggest statue of Luang Pu Thuat at Wat Huai Mongkhon, Hua Hin, Prachuap Khiri Khan

Main Hall of Wat Huai Mongkhon, Prachuap Khiri Khan

Luang Pu Thuat and Elephant Wooden statues at Wat Huai Mongkhon, Hua Hin, Prachuap Khiri Khan

Luang Pu Thuat (Thai: หลวงปู่ทวด), also known as Luang Pu Thuad, born 2125 BE (1582 CE), died 2225 BE (1682 CE) is a revered Buddhist monk who lived in Siam. He is said to have performed miracles.

History

Luang Pu Thuat is mentioned in the early regional histories of southern Thailand, but his life is mainly preserved in oral traditions. Stories of the famous monk were passed on by word of mouth for centuries. As a result, it is a mixture of Buddhist elements: early signs, alleged magic, travel, study, meditation, and eventual "sainthood."

His movements throughout the Southern peninsula constitute a path of pilgrimage for many of his followers.

Amulets

Many people in Thailand, Singapore, and Malaysia believe that amulets created in Luang Pu Thuat's image hold great protective powers granting safety in times of distress, especially saving the lives of believers from seemingly fatal automobile accidents. Phra Archan Tim Dharmataro, abbot of Wat Chang Hai is the pioneer creator of Phra Luang Phor Thuad amulets.

Older, sacred amulets of Pu Thuat are considered priceless and very powerful.

Temples and Statues

Navigation menu

Personal tools

Create account
Log in

Namespaces

Article
Talk

Variants

Actions

Search

Navigation

Main page
Contents
Featured content
Current events
Random article
Donate to Wikipedia

Interaction

Help
About Wikipedia
Community portal
Recent changes
Contact Wikipedia

Toolbox

What links here
Related changes
Upload file
Special pages
Permanent link
Page information
Cite this page

Print/export

Create a book
Download as PDF
Printable version

Languages

ไทย
中文
Edit links
Source http://en.wikipedia.org/wiki/Lu-

Nang Kwak

Mae Nang Kwak luck-bringing charm for shopkeepers in Bangkok

Nang Kwak (Thai: แม่นางกวัก) is a spirit or household divinity of Thai folklore. She brings prosperity.

Iconography

Mae Nang Kwak is represented as a beautiful woman wearing a red dress (not always, but more often than other colors) fashioned in the Thai. She also wears a golden crown on her head and is in the sitting or kneeling position. Her right hand is raised in the Thai way of beckoning a customer, with the palm of the hand pointing downwards. Her left hand is resting on her side or holds a bag full of gold on her lap.

The present iconographic figure of Mae Nang Kwak evolved from Mae Po Sop (แม่โพสพ), the Siamese rice goddess, in recent times. The only difference is that she is not wearing the harvested rice sheaf on her right shoulder. The iconography of these goddesses is based in the Hindu goddess Sri Lakshmi, but their true origins are local and more ancient.

The position of her hand in present-day iconography is quite likely borrowed from the Japanese Maneki Neko beckoning cat.

Symbolism

Mae Nang Kwak is a benevolent spirit. She is deemed to bring luck, especially in the form of money, to the household. She is the patron Deity of all Merchants and Salesmen and can be seen in almost every business establishment in Thailand

Thai people like to have a figurine or cloth poster (called a Pha Yant, or Yantra Cloth) of this goddess in their home or shop, where it is often placed by the shrine. Some people also wear amulets with her figure around the neck, which is a logical development, due to the fact that many people in Thailand must travel around to sell their wares, which makes a portable nang Kwak amulet the obvious choice for such a person.

Legends

Although Nang Kwak is more a figure of popular folklore than a religious deity, there are Buddhist legends that seek to incorporate her into the Buddhist fold.

One Buddhist legend presents Nang Kwak as Nang Supawadee. About 2500 years ago, before or during the time when Buddhism was beginning to spread, in the small town of Michikasandhanakara, in the Indian province of Sawadtii, there was a married couple, Sujidtaprahma and his wife Sumanta, who had a daughter named Supawadee. They were merchants who sold small amounts of wares on the markets, only earning just enough to maintain their small family from day to day. One day, they were discussing their hopes and dreams for the future, and decided that they should try to expand their business to make more profit and begin to think of being able to save something for their old age.

As a result of this conversation, they decided to try to afford to buy a gwian (cart) in order to use to travel with and sell their wares to other towns and villages. They also then brought wares from the other towns to sell in Sawadtii and Michigaasandhanakara when they returned. Sometimes, Supawadee would ask to tag along for the ride, and help them. One day, as Supawadee was helping her parents to sell wares in a distant town, she was lucky to be able to hear a sermon by Phra Gumarn Gasaba Thaera; she was so convinced and moved by his sermon, that she took refuge in the Triple Gem. When Gasaba Thaera saw her faith and devotion, he collected all his powers of thought and concentration, for he was an Arahant, and bestowed blessings of good fortune and luck in salesmanship on Nang Supawadee and her Family.

Another story tells of Nang Kwak living on a higher plane of existence: Nang Kwak was the daughter of *Phu Chao Khao Khiao*, meaning 'Grandfather Lord of the Green Mountain' (*Khao Khiao* which could also mean 'Green Horns'). Phu Chao Khao Khiao was a Lord of the Chatu Maha Rachika realm (one of the lower levels of Heaven - an Asura realm of giants and pretas). His other name is 'Pra Panasabodee', and he is the Lord of the forest and places where wild plants grow. In that time, there was an Asura demon called To Kok Khanak (also known as 'To Anurak'). To Kok Khanak was a good friend of Phu Chao Khao Khiao, who had been attacked by Phra Ram (the hero of Ramakien, Thai version of the Ramayana), who had thrown a Kok tree at him which pierced his chest and carried him through space to be pinned to the side of Pra Sumen. In addition, Pra Ram cursed him with the following magic spell: 'Until your descendants weave a Civara monks robe from lotus petals, and offer it to Pra Sri Ariya Maedtrai (Maitreya the future Buddha) your curse will not be lifted.'

After this, Nang Prachant, the daughter of Lord Kok Khanag had to serve her father, spending the days and nights trying to weave a Civara robe from lotus petals, in order to have it ready for offering to Pra Sri Ariya Maedtrai who will descend to become enlightened in a future age from now. Meanwhile To Kok Khanak had to remain cursed and pinned to Pra Sumen and his daughter was in a dire situation without her father to help run things. Since she had to spend all her time weaving the Civara, she had no time to go sell things or make money, nor time to run a shop. When Jao Khao Khiaw heard the news of this, he felt compassion, and sent his daughter Nang Kwak to go stay with her as a companion. Because of her merit, Nang Kwak caused merchants and rich nobles from around the area to flock to Nang Prachant's home and bestow gifts of gold, silver and money on them. Nang Prachant then became wealthy and led a comfortable life.

Gallery

Mae Nang Kwak figurine at Koon Ngam Ching Yuen(Temple), Hong Kong
Mae Nang Kwak figurine at a shrine in Cha Am
Mae Nang Kwak at Wat Phra That Ruang Rong, Sisaket Province
Source http://en.wikipedia.org/wiki/Nang_Kwak

Nariphon

Thai lacquerwork painting of the Naripon tree at Phra Pathom Chedi

The **Nariphon** (นารีผล), also known as **Makaliphon or Makaliporn** (from Pali *makkaliphala*, Thai: มักกะลีผล, RTGS: *Makkaliphon*) is a tree in Buddhist mythology which bears fruit in the shape of young female creatures. The maidens grow attached by their head from the tree branches. This tree grows at the Himaphan, a mythical forest where the female fruits are enjoyed by the Gandharvas who cut the fruits and take them away.

The Nariphon is also mentioned in the Vessantara Jataka in which Indra placed these trees around the grove where the Bodhisattva Vessantara meditated.

Myths and folklore

According to Buddhist mythology God Indra created a pavilion (*Sala*) as an abode for Vessantara and his wife and two children to live. His wife went into the forest to collect fruits and was in danger of being attacked by Hermits or Yogis who lived in the forest who had not conquered lust, although they had acquired special powers from their meditation. Therefore Indra created twelve of these special Nariphon tree s which would bear fruit whenever she went out to collect food and so distract these men. Being all in the image of Indra's beautiful wife, like sweet-smelling naked sixteen-year-old girls, the men took the fruits to their place of abode and after making love to them would sleep for four months and lose their powers.

According to Thai folklore, since Vessantara and his family have died, the trees bear fruit daily. The special forest, trees and sala will disappear when the Buddha's teachings have become lost, predicted to be five thousand years after his death. When these fruit appear on the trees they are like beautiful 16 year old girls and they will last for seven days, following which they will wither and die if they are not picked up. In the heavenly realms males and females are eternally youthful and, since there is no suffering, there is no ageing. They have same internal organs as humans, but no bones. These maidens have also magic powers and possess spirits which can sing and dance.

There are supposedly two Makaliporn pods in a Buddhist temple near Bangkok. It is said that they came from Himaphan, the mythical forest. At Wat Pheut Udom temple near Pathum Thani there is a representation of the tree together with ghosts and hell-scenes. Representations of the Nariphon tree are very common in Thai comic books, both fresh and dry, often in manga style. Amulets and charms in the form of Nariphon girls are sold throughout Thailand. Folk stories claim that the tree grows somewhere in the Phetchabun Mountains and hoaxes are common; these include pictures of Nariphon girls growing from trees as well as dry Nariphon maidens.

The Nariphon myth inspired the 2006 Thai film Nariphon (นารีผล, "Devil Ivy"), with Chayanan Arjpru, Tassachol Pongpakawat and Paymanee Sangkakorn, and 2010 movie *Nariphon Khon Phriksa* (นารีผล คนพฤกษา, "Nariphon, People from the Tree"), with Phasakon Phomrabut and Thanmon Theklamlong.

Source http://en.wikipedia.org/wiki/Nariphon

Phi Fa

Phi Fa or **Pee Fah** (Thai: ผีฟ้า, Lao: ຜີຟ້າ) is a ghost or spirit of the local folklore of Northeast Thailand (Isan) and Laos. It is also known as *Nang Fa* (นางฟ้า) or *Phi Thaen* (ผีแถน) and is often represented as a woman having a malevolent side, related to the Phi Pop spirit. Phi Fa is believed to bring about disease and natural disasters.

Phi Fa ritual

The Phi Fa Ritual is a practice preferably celebrated for a person that recovers after convalescence from a serious disease. The shaman is the medium, that is able to contact Phi Fa and invite her to take part in the ceremony. The shaman selects the suitable date and location for the ceremony, instructs the people during the preparation of the ritual, controls the correct decoration of the sacrificial altar and conducts the full ceremony.

Music, Chanting and Dancing are indispensable elements of the Phi Fa Ritual. The Khaen, a bamboo mouth organ, is the central music instrument of the ritual. It is creating a sacred atmosphere when used to accompany ritual prayers and devotions and it is engaging the participants of the ritual while leading the rhythmic dancing around the sacrificial altar. Especially for the latter dedication the Khaen is accompanied by the Phing (a guitar like string instrument), by a hand drum and by Chings (small bells, cymbals). The genre of chanting is very similar to Mor lam, the traditional music of Lao and Northeast-Thailand.

The guests of a Phi Fa Ritual involve themselves into this highly spiritual ceremony with dancing around a decorated sacrificial altar. The dance lasts a full night and creates trance conditions for many of the participants. They believe Phi Fa will participate the ceremony and they expect healing and protection from unfavorable fortune.

The steps of the ritual are related to the songs chanted by the shaman and are always accompanied by the Khaen. This is because the Khaen is believed to be an important mean to communicate with the gods and the spirits. The steps of the ritual are as follows: Inviting the gods or spirits, explaining the reason for the invitation, pray for assistance, pray for protection, consoling the patient, recalling the spirit that has fled the patient, inviting Phi Fa to accept the offerings, Baasii ritual, fortune telling and take leave of Phi Fa.

The Baasii Ritual

The baasii ceremony is an important part of Lao culture and few Lao would consider undertaking a long journey or important endeavor without holding one. The faithful sit around a small table on which a variety of offerings are displayed – bananas, sticky rice, biscuits, money and rice whiskey. An elder or a shaman recites the blessing, while everyone touches the offerings or, if they can't reach, the elbow of someone touching the offerings. The elder or the shaman ties a piece of string around the wrist. In Lao tradition, the soul consists of many guardian spirits that occasionally wander away from their owner. These must be called back and bound to the body to ensure a person is properly protected before any important undertaking. Once the elder has finished other participants continue tying loops of string. Yet more string is produced and finally everyone ties string around each other's wrists, whispering good wishes all the while. It is believed that the string must be worn for at least three full days to ensure the desired effect.

Phi Fa dance

Lam Phi Fa (ລາຜີຟ້າ, ลำผีฟ้า, IPA: lam pʰiː faː) is part of the ritual to propitiate spirits in cases of possession. Musically it derived from *Lam Tang Yao*; however, it was performed not by trained musicians but by those (most commonly old women) who were thought themselves to have been cured by the ritual.

In his *Traditional Music of the Lao*, Terry Miller identifies five factors which helped to produce the various genres of *lam* or dance in Isan: animism, Buddhism, story telling, ritual courtship and male-female competitive folksongs; one of these is *Lam Phi Fa*, the Phi Fa dance. *Lam Phi Fa*, together with *Lam Phuen* is one of the oldest genres.

Modern adaptations

Chao Nang, "The Princess's Terror", 1997 Pop Phi Fa and 2009 Pop Phi Fa (remake) are Thai television soap operas (ละคร) based on the Phi Fa / Phi Pop legend.

Source http://en.wikipedia.org/wiki/Phi_Fa

Phi Ta Khon

Phi Ta Khon (also spelled *Pee Ta Khon* (Thai: ผีตาโขน), sometimes known as **Ghost Festival**), is the most common name for a group of festivals held in Dan Sai, Loei province, Isan, Thailand. The events take place over three days some time between March and July, the dates being selected annually by the town's mediums.

The whole event is called *Bun Luang*, part of a Buddhist merit-making holiday also known as *Bun Phawet*.

Ghosts of Phi Ta Khon

Ghosts holding palad khik (penis amulet)

The first day is the Ghost Festival itself, also called *Wan Ruam* (assembly day). The town's residents invite protection from *Phra U-pakut*, the spirit of the Mun river. They then hold a series of games and take part in a procession wearing masks made of rice husks or coconut leaves with hats made from rice steamers, plus patchwork clothing. They also wear bells and wave wooden phalluses.

The origins of this part of the festival are traditionally ascribed to a story of the Vessantara Jataka in which the Buddha in one of his past lives as a prince made a long journey and was presumed dead. The celebrations on his return were so raucous as to wake the dead.

The second day of the festival incorporates elements of the Rocket Festival, plus costume and dance contests and more parades.

On the third and final day, the villagers listen to sermons from Buddhist monks.

Source http://en.wikipedia.org/wiki/Phi_Ta_Khon

Villagers greet the medium (day 2)

Phraya Anuman Rajadhon

Phya Anuman Rajadhon (Thai: พระยาอนุมานราชธน; RTGS: **Phraya Anuman Ratchathon**, also spelled *Phaya Anuman Rajadhon* or *Phrayā Anuman Rajadhon*; December 14, 1888—July 12, 1969), was one of modern Thailand's most remarkable scholars. He was a self-trained linguist, anthropologist and ethnographer that became an authority on Thai culture. His name is **Yong Sathiankoset** (ยง เสฐียรโกเศศ); Phraya Anuman Rajadhon is his noble title. He also took his family name, Sathiankoset, as his pen name by which he is well known.

His prolific work and his interest in a multitude of cultural-related fields, from folklore to sociology, set the foundations for a long-lasting cultural awareness among young Thai scholars.

Phraya Anuman Rajadhon was the first Thai scholar who seriously studied Thai folkloristics and took notes on the nocturnal village spirits of Thai folklore. He established that, since such spirits were not represented in paintings or drawings, they were purely based on popular traditional stories. Thus most of the contemporary iconography of ghosts such as Nang Tani, Nang Takian,

Phya Anuman Rajadhon studied in depth such apparently unimportant details of his culture as the charms used by Thai shopkeepers to attract customers. A Nang Kwak luck-bringing paper from a shop in Bangkok

Krasue, Krahang, Phi Am, Phi Hua Kat, Phi Pop, Phi Phong, Phi Phraya, Phi Tai Hong and Mae Nak has its origins in Thai films that have become classics.

Biography

Moved by an innate curiosity and having an eye for detail, Phya Anuman Rajadhon observed and took notes on the Thai society that surrounded him at the crucial time when much of the traditional culture was being overwhelmed by modernity. As years went by he studied in depth the language, popular customs, oral tradition, social norms and the value system of the Thai people.

He worked in different places, including the Hotel Oriental in Bangkok, during his youth and middle age. In the years when Phya Anuman Rajadhon worked as a clerk at the Thai Customs Department, he got to know a Mr. Norman Mackay who helped him to polish his broken English.

He had no academic titles and did all the training he needed for his research and compilation work humbly, tirelessly and on his own. Phya Anuman Rajadhon took a special interest in popular culture. Many particular ancient habits of Thais he recorded and described would have died unnoticed if they would have not been put down into writing by him. Often his descriptions were accompanied by illustrations.

As a writer he wrote novels under the pen name **Sethyankōsēt**, often spelled as *Sathirakoses*, (Thai: เสฐียรโกเศศ). He also wrote works on important Thai cultural figures, like a biography of Phra Saraprasoet '(Trī Nākhaprathīp)' (1889–1945), a likewise dedicated author and commentator in the field of Thai literature.

Recognition came to Phya Anuman Rajadhon towards his old age, when he was invited to universities to give lectures and began travelling abroad. He was given the post of President of the Siam Society and ended up becoming one of Thailand's most respected intellectuals, both in the last years of his life and posthumously.

The commemoration of the 100th year of his birth was staged in 1988 by UNESCO, where social activist Sulak Sivaraksa, founder of the Sathirakoses-Nagapradeepa Foundation, described Phya Anuman Rajadhon as a National Hero.

Selected works

Only a fraction of Phya Anuman Rajadhon's works have been translated into English.

Essays on Thai Folklore, Editions Duang Kamol, ISBN 974-210-345-3
Popular Buddhism in Siam and other Essays on Thai Studies, Thai Inter-religious Commission on Development and Sathirakoses-Nagapradipa Foundation, Bangkok 1986
Thet Maha Chat. Promotion and Public Relations Sub-Division, Fine Arts Department, Bangkok 1990
Life and Ritual in Old Siam: Three Studies of Thai Life and Customs, New Haven, HRAF Press, 1961
Five papers on Thai custom, Southeast Asia Program, Dept. of Far Eastern Studies, Cornell University, Ithaca, N. Y. 1958
Some traditions of the Thai and other translations of Phya Anuman Rajadhon's articles on Thai customs, Thai Inter-Religious Commission for Development & Sathirakoses-Nagapradipa Foundation, Suksit Siam, Bangkok 1987
The Nature and Development of the Thai Language, Thai Culture, New series; no. 10, Thailand; Fine Arts Dept., Bangkok 1961
Thai Literature in Relation to the Diffusion of Her Cultures, Thailand Culture New Series; no. 9, Thailand; Fine Arts Dept., Bangkok 1969
Thai Language, National Culture Institute, Bangkok 1954
Chao Thi and some traditions of Thai, National Culture Institute, Bangkok 1956
Phra Cedi, Journal of the Siam Society, Bangkok 1952
Thai Literature & Swasdi Raksa, Thailand Culture Series; no. 3, National Culture Institute, Bangkok 1956
Introducing cultural Thailand in outline, Thailand Culture Series; no. 1, Thailand; Fine Arts Dept., Bangkok 2006, ISBN 974-417-810-8
The story of Thai marriage custom, Thailand Culture Series; no. 13, National Culture Institute, Bangkok 1954
Loy Krathong and Songkran festival, The National Culture Institute, Bangkok 1953

Journal articles
Journal of the Siam Society (JSS)
JSS Vol. 38.2c (1951). "The Loi Krathong"
JSS Vol.40.1d (1952) "Phra Cedi"
JSS Vol. 40.2f (1952). "The Ceremony of Tham Khwan of a Month Old Child"
JSS Vol. 41.2c (1954). "The Phi"
JSS Vol. 42.1d (1954). "The Water Throwing"
JSS Vol. 42.1e (1954). "Bathing ceremony"
JSS Vol.42.1f (1954). "Amusements during Songkran festival"
JSS Vol. 42.2b (1955). "The end of Buddhist Lent"
JSS Vol. 43.1e (1955). "A Note on Divination By Ahom Deodhais"
JSS Vol. 43.1f (1955). "Me Posop, the Rice Mother"
JSS Vol. 45.2e (1957). "The Golden Meru"
JSS Vol. 48.2c (1960). "Fertility Rites in Thailand"
JSS Vol. 49.1e (1961). "Some Siamese Superstitions About Trees and Plants"

JSS Vol. 49.2f (1961). "Thai Traditional Salutation"
JSS Vol. 50.2d (1962). "The Khwan and its Ceremonies"
JSS Vol. 52.2d (1964). "Thai Charms and Amulets"
JSS Vol. 53.1h (1965). "Data on Conditioned Poison"
JSS Vol. 53.2b (1965). "A Study on Thai Folk Tale"
JSS Vol. 55.2b (1967). "Notes on the Thread-Square in Thailand"
JSS Vol. 58.1i (1970). "Obituary Phy Anuman Rajadhon"
JSS Vol. 76.0v (1988). "Phya Anuman Rajadhon (Obituary by Somchai Anuman Rajadhon)"
Source http://en.wikipedia.org/wiki/Phraya_Anuman_Rajadhon

Phra Aphai Mani

Aphai Mani statue on Ko Samet

Phra Aphai Mani (Thai: พระอภัยมณี) is a 30,000-line epic written by Thailand's best-known poet, Sunthorn Phu. It is also part of the Thai folklore and has been adapted into films and comics.

Plot

Two princes get banned from Rattana by their father, King Sudas. During their journey, one of the brothers, Aphai Mani, is seduced by a beautiful woman who changes into a sea ogress (นางผีเสื้อสมุทร) when she becomes jealous after he fell in love with a mermaid. His brother Sri Suvan and a couple of warriors want to rescue him.

Phra Aphai Mani in modern popular culture

There are a few Thai films based on this popular legend, including The Adventure of Sudsakorn and the Legend of Sudsakorn.

There is also a Thai comic series with the name Apaimanee Saga.

On some locations in Thailand such as Ko Samet island and Cha Am there are statues related to the Phra Aphai Mani story.

Source http://en.wikipedia.org/wiki/Phra_Aphai_Mani

Phra Mae Thorani

Translations of

Phra Mae Thorani

Pali:	Vasudhara
Burmese:	Wathondare (????????)
	Wathondara (????????)
Khmer:	Preah Thorani
Pwo Karen:	Soung Th' Rui
Thai:	Phra Mae Thorani (พระแม่ธรณี)
	Mae Phra Thorani (แม่พระธรณี)
	Nang Thorani (นางธรณี)

Glossary of Buddhism

Phra Mae Thorani (Thai: พระแม่ธรณี), **Mae Phra Thorani** (Thai: แม่พระธรณี) or **Nang Thorani** (นางธรณี), known as **Wathondara** (????????) or **Wathondare** (????????) in Burmese, from Pali **Vasudhara**) are Thai and Lao language

Phra Mae Thorani bronze statuette. Bangkok National Museum

names for the Khmer language **Preah Thorani**, an earth goddess of the Buddhist mythology of the region. She is also known as **Suvathara** or **Sowathara**.

Etymology

The word "*Thorani*" is the Royal Thai General System of Transcription romanization of "*dharaṇī*", a loanword from Pali and Sanskrit for ground, earth and *Phra*, from the Pali *Vara* and the Thai *Mae* (mother).

Iconography and symbology

Painting in a Laotian monastery. Buddha during the Battle with Mara pointing towards the earth summoning Phra Mae Thorani to come to his assistance.

Images of Phra Mae Thorani are common in shrines and Buddhist temples of

Wat Phnom mural, Phnom Penh, Cambodia Phra Mae Thorani placing herself between the demons and the Buddha

Burma, Cambodia, Thailand and Laos. According to Buddhist myths Phra Mae Thorani is personified as a young woman wringing the cool waters of detachment out of her hair, to drown Mara, the demon sent to tempt the Buddha as he meditated under the bodhi tree.

In temple murals Phra Mae Thorani is often depicted with the Buddha in the posture of Calling the earth to witness. The waters flowing forth from her long hair wash away the armies of Mara and symbolize the water of the bodhisattva's perfection of generosity *(dana parami)*.

" 'The Bodhisattva was sitting in meditation on his throne under the Bodhi Tree, Mara, the Evil One, was jealous and wanted to stop him from reaching enlightenment. Accompanied by his warriors, wild animals and his daughters, he tried to drive the Bodhisattva from his throne. All the gods were terrified and ran away, leaving the Bodhisattva alone to face Mara's challenge. The Bodhisattva stretched down his right hand and touched the earth, summoning her to be his witness. The earth deity in the form of a beautiful woman rose up from underneath the throne, and affirmed the Bodhisattva's right to occupy the vajriisana. She twisted her long hair, and torrents of water collected there from the innumerable donative libations of the Buddha over the ages created a flood. The flood washed away Mara and his army, and the Bodhisattva was freed to reach enlightenment. "

"Touching the earth"

Calling the earth to witness

In the Iconography of Gautama Buddha in Laos and Thailand, "Touching the earth" refers to the Buddha's pointing towards the earth, to summon the Earth Goddess to come to his assistance in obtaining enlightenment, by witnessing to his past good deeds.

Phra Mae Thorani fountain in Bangkok

Buddhist water libation

In Burmese Buddhism, the water libation ceremony, called (*yay zet cha*),

Photograph of a libation ceremony in 1900.

which involves the ceremonial pouring of water from a glass into a vase, drop by drop, concludes most Buddhist ceremonies including donation celebrations and feasts. This ceremonial libation is done to share the accrued merit with all other living beings in all 31 planes of existence. While the water is poured, a confession of faith, called the *hsu taung imaya dhammanu*, is recited and led by the monks. Then, the merit is distributed by the donors, called *ahmya wei* by saying *Ahmya ahmya ahmya yu daw mu gya ba gon law* three times, with the audience responding *thadu*, Pali for "well done." The earth goddess Vasudhara is invoked to witness these meritorious deeds. Afterward, the libated water is poured on soil outside, to return the water to Vasudhara.

Modern use as a symbol

Phra Mae Thorani is featured in the logo of:
The Bangkok Metropolitan Waterworks Authority.
The Democrat Party (Thailand) to emphasise the importance of earth and water for Thailand, together with the Pali proverb *sachamwe amatta wacha* (สจฺจํเว อมตา วาจา) "truth is indeed the undying word," to symbolise the values of the Party.
Mae Thorani may also appear as a decorative element of Thai folklore.

Source http://en.wikipedia.org/wiki/Phra_Mae_Thorani

Rocket Festival

Phaya Thaen Park *Saen* launch racks, Yasothon, Thailand

A **Rocket Festival** (Thai: ประเพณีบุญบั้งไฟ Prapheni Bun Bang Fai , Lao: ບຸນບັ້ງໄຟ Bun Bang Fai') is a merit-making ceremony traditionally practiced by ethnic Lao people throughout much of northeast Thailand and Laos, in numerous villages and municipalities near the beginning of the rainy season. Celebrations typically include preliminary music and dance performances, competitive processions of floats, dancers and musicians on the second day, and culminating on the third day in competitive firings of home-made rockets. Local participants and sponsors use the occasion to enhance their social prestige, as is customary in traditional Buddhist folk festivals throughout Southeast Asia.

History

These Buddhist festivals are presumed to have evolved from pre-Buddhist fertility rites held to celebrate and encourage the coming of the rains, from before the 9th Century discovery of black powder. This festival displays some earthy elements of Lao folklore. Coming immediately prior to the planting season, the festivals offer an excellent chance to make merry before the hard work begins; as well as enhancing communal prestige, and attracting and redistributing wealth as in any Gift culture.

Scholars study the centuries old rocket festival tradition today as it may be significant to the history of rocketry in the East, and perhaps also significant in the postcolonial socio-political development of the Southeast Asian nation states. Economically, villages and sponsors bear the costs in many locations in Laos and in northern Isan (Northeast Thailand). The festivals typically begin at the beginning of the rainy season, in the sixth or seventh lunar months.

Anthropology Professor Charles F. Keyes advises, "In recognition of the deep-seated meaning of certain traditions for the peoples of the societies of mainland Southeast Asia, the rulers of these societies have incorporated some indigenous symbols into the national cultures that they have worked to construct in the postcolonial period. Giving the "Bun Bang Fai or fire rocket festival of Laos" as one example, he adds that it remains "…far more elaborate in the villages than in the cities…."

Today

Today, it is not so likely for the villages to stage "Bun Bang Fai" more elaborate than highly promoted Yasothon's. However, even villages may have themed floats conveying government messages, as Keyes advises. They may also include fairs. In recent years the Tourism Authority of Thailand has helped promote these events, particularly the festivals in the Thai provinces of Nong Khai and Yasothon—the latter boasting the largest and most elaborate of these festivals.

Yasothon's festival

Since the March 1, 1972, separation of Yasothon from Ubon Ratchathani Province, with its world-famous Candle Festival, Yasothon's provincial capital has elaborately staged its now world-famous Rocket Festival annually over the Friday, Saturday and Sunday weekend that falls in the middle of May.

Raw Friday (Thai: วันศุกร์ดิบ, Wan Sook Dip) features all-night performances of **Mor Lam Sing** (Thai–Isan: หมอลำซิ่ง), which continue intermittently into the wee hours of Monday. Mor Lam Sing is a type of *morlam* that is very popular among the local Isan-Lao population. The performance goes on

Village Mor Lam Sing

all night and the locals have great fun. Outsiders have a hard time understanding the humour, which is often rather bawdy.

Bang Fai Ko on Yasothon float before the parade.

Dancers in Yasothon parade.

Saturday brings on the competitions for **Hae Bangfai Ko** (Thai: แห่บั้งไฟโก้). *"Hàe"* are street parades or demonstrations usually featuring traditional dance and accompanying musicians, typically with khaen (Thai: แคน), Gongs, Lao-Isan Klong Yao (Thai: กลองยาว), *long drum*), and an electric guitar, powered by an inverter and car batteries in a handcart that also mounts horn loudspeakers.

Bangfai Ko are richly decorated rockets mounted on traditional but highly decorated oxcarts, or modern floats. Most but not all bold *Bangfai Ko* are for show and not actually capable of flight. Many sport the heads of Nāgas; if equipped with water pumps and swivels, they *are* actually capable of spitting on spectators.

The principal theme of any *Hae Bangfai* is the Phadaeng and Nang Ai legend (below), so many floats (or highly decorated oxcarts) also depict the couple and their retinue. Other modern themes present as well, as suggested by Keyes (ibid.) Participating groups compete for prizes within their categories. *Hàe* typically end in a wat, where dancers and accompanying musicians may further compete in traditional folk dance. All groups prominently display the names of their major sponsors.

Rocket Festival Cameraman

Recalling the fertility rite origins of the festival, parade ornaments and floats often sport phallic symbols and imagery.

Shoots: note phallus protruding from "camera"

Amid the festive atmosphere, dirty humour is widespread.

Festivities also include cross-dressing, both cross-sex and cross-generational, and great quantities of alcohol. Perhaps the most popular beverage, both because it is cheaper than beer and has a higher, 40-percent alcohol content, is a neutral grain spirit called **Sura** (Thai: สุรา), but more generally known as *Lao Whiskey* (Thai: เหล้าลาว, *Lao lao* in Laos and *Lao Khao* (Thai: เหล้าขาว, *white alcohol*) in Thailand. Sato (Thai: สาโท), a brewed rice beverage similar to Japanese sake, may also be on offer; sweet-flavored *sato* may be as little as seven-percent alcohol, but it packs a surprising punch.

Sunday competition moves on to the launching of Bangfai, judged, in various categories, for apparent height and distance travelled, with extra points for exceptionally beautiful vapor trails Those whose rockets misfire are either covered with mud, or thrown into a mud puddle (that also serves a safety function, as immediate application of cooling mud can reduce severity of burns). While popular and entertaining, the festival is also dangerous, with participants and spectators alike occasionally being injured or even killed. On May 10, 1999, a *Lan* 120 kg rocket exploded 50 meters above ground, just two seconds after launch, killing five persons and wounding 11.

Bang Fai (the rockets)

Rocket on ascent.

Jaruat (Thai: จรวด) is the proper term for rockets used as missiles or weapons, but **Bang Fai** (Thai: บั้งไฟ) skyrockets are gigantic black-powder bottle rockets. Tiny bottle rockets are so-called because they may be launched from a bottle. In the case of the similar appearing *Bang Fai*, also spelled 'Bong Fai' (Thai: บ้องไฟ), the 'bottle' is a *bong* (Thai: บ้อง), a section of bamboo Culm used as a container or pipe (and only colloquially as a pipe for smoking marijuana.)

Bangfai Meun showing wooden nozzle

Related to the Chinese Fire Arrow, Bang Fai are made from bamboo bongs. Most contemporary ones, however, are enclosed in pvc piping, making them less dangerous by standardizing their sizes and black-powder charges (which contest rules require be compounded by the rocketeers, themselves). Baking or boiling a bong kills insect eggs that otherwise hatch in dead bamboo and eat it, inside out. Skipping this step may cause the bong to disintegrate and melt the pvc piping. Vines tie long bamboo tails to launching racks. The time it takes for the exhaust to burn through the vines (usually) allows a motor to build up to full thrust; then the tails impart in-flight stability. Ignition comes from a burning fuse or electric match.

Bang Fai come in various sizes, competing in several categories. Small ones are called Bang Fai **Noi** (Thai: น้อย). Larger categories are designated by the counting words for 10,000, 100,000 and 1,000,000: *Meun* (Thai: หมื่น) "Saen" (Thai: แสน) and the largest Bang Fai, the *Lan* (Thai: ล้าน). These counting words see use in many contexts to indicate increasing size or value. *Lan* in this context may be taken to mean *extremely large* as well as extremely expensive and extremely dangerous: *Bang Fai Lan* are nine metres long and charged with 120 kg of black powder. These may reach altitudes reckoned in kilometers, and travel dozens of kilometers down range (loosely speaking, as they can go in any direction, including right through the crowd). Competing rockets are scored for apparent height, distance, and beauty of the vapor trail (Thai: ไอ). A few include skyrocket pyrotechnics. A few also include parachutes for tail assemblies, but most fall where they may.

Nang Ai, Phadaeng, and Phangkhi

Phadaeng and Nang Ai

Nang Ai (Thai: นางไอ่), in full, **Nang Ai Kham** (นางไอ่คำ) is queen of the pageant and **Phadaeng** (ผาแดง) is her champion. She is famed as the most beautiful girl. He, an outsider, comes to see for himself, lavishes her with gifts and wins her heart; but must win a rocket festival tournament to win her hand. Unwittingly, he becomes part of a love triangle.

Phangkhi

Phangkhi (ภังคี) and Nang Ai have been fated by their Karma (กรรม *kam*) to have been reborn throughout many past existences as soul mates (คู่สร้าง *khusang*, Lao-Isan สายแนนนำเกี่ยว *sai naen nam kiaw*.) Stories about the couple, however, say they have not exactly been lovers: in many a past existence, she has been a dutiful wife, but would not yield an inch in an argument to anyone (ไม่ยอมใคร *mai yom krai*) and he only wanted to satisfy himself (เอาแต่ใจตัวเอง *ow dtae jai dtua eng*). She becomes fed up and prays never to be paired with him, ever again. Nang Ai is reborn as the daughter of *Phraya Khom* (พระยาขอม, (which means Lord Khmer; but even if her father was a Cambodian overlord, *Nang Ai Kham* is still the genuine article), while Phangki is reborn as the son of Phaya Nak, the Grand Nāga who rules the Deeps. (He is depicted in parades in the guise of a prince, riding alone, dogging the new pair.) Phangki isn't invited to the tournament, and Phadaeng's rocket fizzles. Nang Ai's uncle is the winner, so her father calls the whole thing off, which is considered to be a very bad omen, indeed. Pangkhii shape-shifts into a white squirrel to spy on Nang Ai, but she espies him and has him killed by a royal hunter. Pangkhii's flesh magically transforms into meat equal to 8,000 cartloads. Nang Ai and many of her countrymen ate of this tainted flesh, and Phaya Nak vows to allow no one to remain living who had eaten of the flesh of his son. Aroused from the Deeps, he and his watery myrmidons rise and turn the land into a vast swamp. Nagas personify waters running both above and below ground, and nagas run amok are rivers in spate: all Isan is flooded.

Phadaeng flees the rising flood with Nang Ai on his white stallion, *Bak Sam* (บักสาม Mr. Three), but she is swept off by a Naga's tail, not to be seen again. (Bak Sam is seen in parades sporting his stallion's equipage (อวัยวะเพศของม้า *awaiyawa pet kong ma*) that legend says dug a lick called *Lam Huay Sam* (ลำห้วยสาม, which may be seen to this day in Ban Sammo-Nonthan, Tambon Pho Chai, Amphoe Khok Pho Chai. The legend also tells that receding waters left behind the Nong Han Kumphawapi Lake of the Kumphawapi District marsh, which, too, may be seen to this very day.) Phadaeng escapes, but pines away for his lost love. His ghost then raises an army of the spirits of the air to wage war on the nagas below. The war continues until both sides are exhausted, and the dispute is submitted to King Wetsawan (ท้าวเวสสุวรรณ), king of the North, for arbitration. His decision: the cause of the feud has long since been forgotten and all disputants must let bygones be bygone.

The legend is retold in many regional variations, all of which are equally true for they relate events in different existences. One 3000-word poem translated to English from this rich Thai-Isan tradition, "…is especially well known to the Thai audience, having been designated as secondary school supplementary reading by the Thai Ministry of Education, with publication in 1978. There is even a Thai popular song about the leading characters." The original was written in a Lao-Isan verse called Khong saan, replete with sexual innuendo, puns, and double entendre.

Keyes (op. cit., p. 67, citing George Coedès) p. 48, says "Phra Daeng Nang Ai" is a version of the Kaundinya, legendary founder of Funan; and Soma, the daughter of the king of the Nāga. Keyes also wrote that such legends may prove a valuable source of toponyms.

The Myth of the Toad King

Almost everyone, native and visitor alike, will say Bang Fai are launched to bring rain, as in the Tourism Authority of Thailand link, below. However, a careful reading of the underlying myth, as presented in Yasothon and Nong Khai, implies the opposite: the rains bring on the rockets. Their version of the myth:

When the Lord Buddha was in his

Phaya Thaen Park Rocket Shoot

bodhisatta (Pali) (Thai: โพธิสัตว์, *phothisat*) incarnation as **King of the Toads Phaya Khang Khok** (Thai: พญาคางคก), and married to **Udon Khuruthawip** (Thai: อุดรคุรุทวิป, Northern Partner-Knowing-Continent), his sermons drew everyone, creatures and sky-dwellers alike, away from **Phaya Thaen** (Thai: พญาแถน), King of the Sky). Angry Phaya Thaen withheld life-giving rains from the earth for seven years, seven months and seven days. Acting against the advice of the Toad King, **Phaya Naga** (Thai: พญานาค *Phayanak*), King of the Nāga (and personification of the Mekong) declared war on Phaya Thaen—and lost.

King Toad leading war with Phaya Thaen

Persuaded by Phaya Naga to assume command, King Toad enlisted the aid of termites to build mounds reaching to the heavens, and of venomous scorpions and centipedes to attack Phaya Thaen's feet, and of hornets for air support. Previous attempts at aerial warfare against Phaya Thaen in his own element had proved futile; but even the Sky must come down to the ground. On the ground the war was won, and Phaya Thaen sued for peace. Naga Rockets fired in the air at the end of the hot, dry season are not to threaten Phaya Thaen, but to serve as a reminder to him of his treaty obligations made to Lord Bodhisatta Phaya Khang Khok, King of the Toads, down on the ground. For his part Phaya Nak was rewarded by being given the duty of Honor Guard at most Thai and Lao temples.

Naga guarding the Viang Chan, Laos, Temple of Wat Sisaket, itself a survivor of an intemperate war in 1827

Wow tanoo ready to fly

After the harvest of the resulting crops, **Wow thanoo** (Thai: ว่าวธนู, bow kite), man-sized kites with a strung bow, are staked out in winter monsoon winds. They are also called **Túi-tiù** (Thai: ตุ้ยตุ่ย, singing kite), from the sound of the bowstring singing in the wind, which sing all through the night, to signal Phaya Thaen that he has sent enough rain.

All participants (including a wow thanoo) were depicted on murals on the front of the former Yasothon Municipal Bang Fai Museum, but were removed when it was remodeled as a learning centre.

An English-language translation of a Thai report on *Bang Fai Phaya Nark Naga fireballs* at Nong Khai gives essentially the same myth (without the hornets and wow) from Thai folk : The knowledge of Thai life-style . For an alternate English-language version, see Tossa, Wajuppa and Phra 'Ariyānuwat ; *Phya Khankhaak, the Toad King: A Translation of an Isan Fertility Myth in Verse* ; Lewisburg : Bucknell University Press London ; Cranbury, NJ : Associated University Presses ©1996 ISBN 0-8387-5306-X.

Etymology

Bun (Lao: wikt:ບຸນ, Thai: บุญ) merit (Buddhism) is from Pali Puñña merit, meritorious action, virtue, and Sanskrit पुण्य puṇya virtuous or meritorious act, good or virtuous works.

Bang (Lao: wikt:ບັ້ງ, Thai: บั้ง) (alternative spelling *bong* บ้อง,) is a cutting, specifically of bamboo.

Fai (Lao: ໄຟ, Thai: ไฟ), is Fire (classical element).

Prapheni Thai: ประเพณี), tradition, is from Sanskrit परंपर *parampara*, an uninterrupted series, regular series, succession 'to be handed down in regular succession'; from Pali paramparā 7795 paramparā series, tradition.

In popular culture

The 2006 Thai martial arts film, *Kon Fai Bin*, depicts the Rocket Festival. Set in 1890s Siam, the movie's hero, Jone Bang Fai ("Fireball Bandit"), is an expert at building the traditional bamboo rockets, which he uses in conjunction with Muay Thai martial arts to defeat his opponents.

Thai political protests in April 2010

Ruesi

similarly had Red Shirts firing *bang fai* in downtown Bangkok.

Source http://en.wikipedia.org/wiki/Rocket_Festival

Ruesi

Ruesi is the Thai name (Thai: ฤๅษี) for a hermit sage (known as Rishi in India). He is a figure of many legends and stories of the Thai folklore.

The Ruesi are Hermit sages who spend their time meditating and developing psychic powers and collecting magical herbs, minerals, rarities and other substances. They use the magical ingredients to make special love charms, spells and protective amulets. They wish to help other beings to be happier in life, and do this by telling fortunes, making rituals and spells to reduce bad karma, chase evil influences and spirits away, protect from ones enemies, or even increase one's luck and wealth with a spell for wealth and good fortune. Some Rishi wear a reddish brown robe, whereas some even wear white like the Prahm. Some wear white and devote themselves exclusively to healing medical ailments. This kind of Ruesi is known as Chiwok, named after the Rishi Chivaka who was the official doctor of the Lord Buddha. A Chiwok Ruesi would collect herbs minerals and healing substances for making his healing potions. This kind of Ruesi can perhaps be compared to the druid bards who were also healers, using herbal potions and ointments. A Chiwok Ruesi will also be expert in orthopedic massage, and other matters, such as Horoscope.

Of the types of Ruesi who make Sak Yant, most will be of the Dabos variety, such as Ajarn Thoy Dabos (there are many other subcategories of Ruesi within the main variety who wear reddish robes). The Dabos will sometimes also wear a tiger skin over his red robe, because of the tiger skin worn by Lord Shiva, who was and is the original Maha Ruesi (great Ruesi). A Dabos Ruesi will normally have at least one Ruesi mask of the Thai Deity "Ruesi Por Gae Dta Fai" on his altar.

Ruesi Mask

Ruesi masks are called "Siarn Ruesi" is a life sized mask and head dress of an ancient hermit sage (perhaps the Western comparison might be "wizard"). The mask has an open mouth with two big buck teeth sticking out, a beard and long moustache and three eyes. The third eye is located in the centre of the forehead. Ruesi Por Gae is seen as the "Kroo" (master teacher) of all Samnak Sak Yant . The Kroo protects you as a devotee of the lineage of his teachings. Most devotees will receive the Yant Kroo as their first tattoo, this is the bonding process between the devotee and the lineage of Por Gae down from the legendary ancient Ruesi himself right up to his current lineage of Ajarn Sak Yant who have learned his teachings in the lineage from mouth to ear. Some Ruesi (and Prahm) Masters will even become a "Rang Song" (spirit medium) for Por Gae or another spirit Deity to enter them whilst receiving devotees and administering Sak Yant and other magical services. In this case the master will let the Deity use his body to manifest his mind onto this plane and then perform the tattooing or ceremonies directly. In this case, many Ruesi (such as the Ruesi Ajarn Thoy Dabos Por Gae Dta Fai), will don the mask of Por Gae covering their eyes and face whilst tattooing the Yant on the devotee. This renders the Master completely blind as far as seeing the tattoo is concerned, and is seen as yet another proof of the sacred magic of Por Gae Dta Fai, and Sak Yant Tattoos. Many devotees of Sak Yant are also devotees of Por Gae Dta Fai, and will attend the days of reverence to Por Gae, receive his blessing and protection, as well as having the mask of Por Gae placed on his head. This placing of the mask on the head of the devotee is known as "Korb Kroo."

The Ruesi in Modern Times

Most of the Ruesi in modern Thailand are of the "Dabos" type, and are not required to keep vows of sexual abstinence or poverty. Indeed, modern Ruesi often have a nice car, mobile phone, are married, and have children. The only requirement for such Ruesi is that of magical knowledge and psychic ability (having developed these qualities in meditative states).

Almost all Ruesi in Thailand practice the art of magical tattooing, known as *Sak Yant*. Sak Yant is the study and practice of Sacred Geometry in the form of Buddhist and Animist traditions. These Sacred Yantra are said to possess miraculous powers to heal and protect an a host of other purposes

citations

Sak Yant Buddhist Tattoos (e-book)

Author; Spencer Littlewood,(Bangkok)
Publisher; Spencer Littlewood
Chapter 4, Page 4

Related links

Navigation menu

Personal tools

Create account
Log in

Namespaces

Article
Talk

Variants

Actions

Search

Navigation

Main page
Contents
Featured content

Sangsilchai

Sangsilchai (Thai: สังข์ศิลป์ชัย) is an epic poem written in Thailand in 1649 by Thao Phang Kham. The story is based on Thai folklore and displays the principles of Buddhism. The original displays the knowledge of Sanskrit and Pali language of the writer.

Source http://en.wikipedia.org/wiki/Sangsilchai

Suvannamaccha

A mural painting of Suvannamaccha and Hanuman at Wat Phra Kaew, Bangkok.

Suvannamaccha luck bringing charm in a riverside shop in Nonthaburi, Thailand

Suvannamaccha (lit. golden mermaid) is a daughter of Tosakanth (Ravana) that appears in the Cambodian and Thai versions of the Ramayana. Alternative transliterations of her name include *Sovann Maccha* (Khmer: សុវណ្ណមច្ឆា), *Suphanna Matcha* (Thai: นางสุพรรณมัจฉา), *Suvarnamacha* and *Suvannamaccha*.

She is a mermaid princess who tries to spoil Hanuman's plans to build a bridge to Lanka but falls in love with him instead.

The figure of Suvannamaccha is popular in Thai folklore and is represented on small cloth streamers or framed pictures that are hung as luck bringing charms in shops and houses throughout Thailand.

Story

Hanuman, building a causeway, discovered that he was hampered by mermaids underwater. Hanuman is the famous Vanar God of Hindu mythology, the son of Vayu (wind god). When Queen Sita is kidnapped her husband Rama enlists Hanuman's aid in rescuing her.

Hanuman learns that Sita is being held captive on the island of Sri Lanka. He informs King Rama, her husband, who orders him to build a causeway to Sri Lanka from India so Rama's army can attack. Hanuman collects his band of Vanaras and they begin throwing huge boulders into the sea to make a foundation for the causeway.

After a few days they notice something is wrong and call Hanuman to report. They tell him that each day they throw rocks into the sea and the next day they are gone.

Hanuman asks for volunteers to join him while he instructs the others to continue throwing rocks into the sea. When several volunteers have stepped forward Hanuman leads them into the waves. They find a large number of mermaids underwater. As they watch, a new rock is tossed in. The mermaids underwater take the rock and carry it away!

Angrily, Hanuman looks for their leader. He spots an especially lovely mermaid supervising the others. He swims towards her but she skillfully evades him. Time and again he begins an attack but it comes to nothing.

Maybe it starts as respect for the mermaid's abilities, maybe it is the result of her beauty, in either case Hanuman finds he is falling in love with the creature. He changes his tactics and begins to silently woo her. She responds to him and soon they are together at the bottom of the sea.

Later, Hanuman asks the mermaid why she is stealing the rocks. She tells him that she is Suvannamaccha, a daughter of Ravana (the demon who had abducted Sita). When Ravana saw Hanuman's Vanaras building a causeway he instructed Suvannamaccha to stop it. Hanuman tells the mermaid why he is building the causeway. He tells her of the abduction of Queen Sita. The battle between Rama and her father Ravana. He tells her how is he had defied Rama's orders before, and in consequence was ordered to finish the causeway within seven days or pay with his life.

Suvannamaccha turned to Hanuman and her eyes were filled with love. No more, she said, would she prevent Hanuman from completing his mission. Her mermaids underwater would, in fact, return all the stolen rocks to the causeway.

They parted as lovers part but it was not to be the end for them. Hanuman had left a seed with Suvannamaccha and soon she would give birth to their son named Mudchanu.

Source http://en.wikipedia.org/wiki/Suvannamaccha

Thens

Thens are gods or spirits worshipped in Tai folklore, predominantly Lao. They play a prominent role in the Phra Lak Phra Lam and the stories of Khun Borom.

In Laos and Northern Thailand the origins of human society, practical skills and culture are attributed to three divine ancestors, the Thens, and three earthly ancestors, who are sometimes known simply as the three great men.

Source http://en.wikipedia.org/wiki/Thens

The Twelve Sisters

Statue of a female yak (yaksha) or ogress (Thai: ยักษ์; Pali: *Yakkhini*), one of the main characters of this story

Background

The legend of **The Twelve Sisters** or **The Twelve Ladies**, known as *Nang Sip Song* (นางสิบสอง) or as *Phra Rot Meri* (พระรถเมรี) in Thai and as *Puthisen Neang Kong Rei* in Khmer, is a Southeast Asian folktale based on an apocryphal Jātaka Tale, the Rathasena Jātaka of the Paññāsjātaka collection. It is one of the stories of the previous lives of Buddha in which Rathasena, the son of one of the twelve women, is the bodhisattva.

Background

The story of the Twelve Sisters is part of the folk tradition of certain countries in Southeast Asia such as Thailand, Cambodia and Laos and the folktales derived from it come in different versions, often under different titles depending from the country. This legend was also brought to Malaysia by the Malaysian Siamese where it became popular among the Malaysian Chinese community.

It is a long story about the life of twelve sisters abandoned by their parents and adopted by an ogress (Lao *Sundara*; Khmer: *Santhomea*; Thai: *Santhumala*) disguised as a beautiful lady. The conclusion is the sad love story about the only surviving son of the twelve sisters, *Rathasena* (Thai: *Phra Rothasen* พระรถเสน; Khmer: *Rithisen* or *Puthisen*; Lao: *Putthasen*) with *Manora* (Thai: *Meri* เมรี; Lao: *Kankari*; Khmer: *Kong Rei*), the adopted daughter of ogress *Sundara*. At the end both died together upon the long and lonely shore of a lake.

Thai version

A long time ago, there was a rich merchant and his beautiful wife who lived happily in a big house. Despite their good fortune, the couple didn't have any children. One day, they went together to a shrine and made an offering of twelve banana hands to a tree spirit. Not long thereafter the wife became pregnant and the rich man wished with all his might that the child would be a boy, but his wife gave birth to a girl. His wife, however, conceived again and again. She became pregnant twelve times and each time she had a daughter. By that time his business started to go wrong for him since the ships that took his goods to sell in another country were robbed several times. Finally the rich merchant ended up borrowing a lot of money from his friends trying to fix his business problems. Yet, no matter what he did, his family kept getting poorer.

The former rich man found it hard having so many mouths to feed. So he made a plan to abandon his daughters in the forest. He hid this plan from his wife but his youngest daughter named Phao heard about it. When their father left them alone in the deep forest, the twelve girls were able to find their way back home thanks to their younger sister who had left marks in the path. But their father tried again and this time they were not able to find their way back home.

They spent days walking deeper and deeper into the forest and became very hungry. Their father had given them twelve packets of rice, but when they opened them they found out that eleven of them were filled with sand and only one had rice in it. They shared that little rice and ate it crying, lamenting their misfortune. Wandering aimlessly the twelve girls came to a lake, where they tried to catch fish to satiate their hunger. Each of the sisters succeeded in catching a fish and eleven of them playfully poked the eyes of their fish with sharp twigs, except for the youngest one who poked only one eye.

Finally they arrived to the yaksha kingdom, where an ogress named Santhumala saw the exhausted and emaciated girls resting under a tree and decided to adopt them. The ogress transformed herself into a human being, a pleasant-looking woman, and brought the twelve sisters to her home. For many years she treated them as her own daughters and under her care the twelve girls grew up into beautiful young women.

One day, while Santhumala was away hunting, the twelve sisters met an old man who told them that Santhumala was not a human, but an ogress who liked to eat young women like them. So they fled from the ogre kingdom and wandered for days until they arrived to a clear river where they took a bath to refresh themselves. The local king saw the twelve ladies playing in the water and fell in love with them. So he brought them to his palace and married the twelve sisters.

When Santhumala came back to her home and found that the girls were gone, she flew into a rage. She quickly found out where they were and transformed herself into a very beautiful young woman, more beautiful than any of the twelve sisters; then she went to the city of the king and asked to meet him. The king was spellbound by Santhumala's beauty and swiftly married her, promoting her to the rank of first queen. Jealous of the king's favoritism, the Twelve Sisters were not kind to the new queen. Although they were polite to her in front of the king, they were often mean to her in private. To take her revenge from the Twelve Sisters, Santhumala, the favorite queen, feigned sickness and the king became worried. She told the king that the cause of her disease was the ill-treatment of the twelve other wives and the only thing that would heal her would be a medicine distilled from the eyes of the Twelve Sisters.

The king was so infatuated with Santhumala that he assented. Under his orders eleven of his wives had both of their eyes gouged out, but the youngest one had had only one eye removed. Following this the Twelve Sisters were banished to a deep dark cave from where there was no way out. Then the king instructed his servants not to bring any food and not to help the Twelve Sisters in any way.

All the twelve sisters were pregnant and they all successively gave birth to babies but all died. Since the women were being starved under Santhumala's strict orders, each one chopped her baby's body into twelve pieces to share with the other sisters to eat. When Phao gave birth to a beautiful boy who was alive, she lied to her sisters that her son was dead. Phao named her son Rothasen and looked after him well. As he grew he found a secret way out of the deep cave. He had a cock that won in all the cockfights. With the prize money he bought rice and from then onward he brought regularly food for his mother and his eleven aunts. As years went by Rothasen became a handsome young man. When the king heard of him, he invited him to the palace where he played games of dice with the monarch displaying great skill.

Santhumala found out that twelve sisters were alive and she was angry that her plan to get rid had failed. Again she feigned sickness and told the king that only a certain fruit growing in her kingdom could cure her. She also told the king that only Phra Rothasen would be able to fetch it. So she wrote the following letter to her adoptive daughter, Meri, in the language of the ogres: *"If this young man arrives to our kingdom in the morning, devour him in the morning; but if he arrives in the night, devour him in the night"*

On the way to the kingdom Phra Rothasen met an old Rshi who gave him a flying horse named Pachi to ride and who gave him hospitality. While the boy slept the sage altered the meaning of the letter by replacing the words "devour him" with "marry him".

Thus, when he arrived at the kingdom of the ogres Phra Rothasen went straight to Meri and showed her the letter. Meri was surprised and pleased at seeing the virtuous-looking and handsome young man and she fell in love with him, celebrating her wedding with him straight away as directed.

Meri was a kind-hearted and beautiful lady and Phra Rothasen lived with her very happily for some time, but he remembered his blind mother and aunts who still stayed in the dark cave. While showing him the palace, Meri had told Rothasen about certain magic medicines kept in a locked room including Phra Rothasen's mother and aunts's eyes. Then he made a plan to get Meri to sleep by making her drink wine and take the eyes for his mother and aunts. Thus one night, after Meri was sleeping, Phra Rothasen stole many medicines and the eyes from the locked room. Meri woke up and looked for her husband but she saw him far away riding his flying horse. She suddenly grew into a giant and followed Phra Rothasen crying and calling him with a loud voice. To stop her, Phra Rothasen threw a magic branch that turned the space between them into a deep lake and a high mountain. Seeing her husband escape from her Meri wailed in despair, asking him to stop. Phra Rothasen was moved by her sad screams and replied that he will back after he finished his urgent mission. Then Phra Rothasen flew away and left Meri with a broken heart crying bitterly at the shore of the lake.

Phra Rothasen arrived back to his city and killed evil Santhumala with a magic club. He then went into the deep dark cave and healed the eyes of his mother and aunts by putting them back in their place with a special magic ointment. His mother and aunts left their deep cave and regained their former status with the king. They invited him to live in the palace again but Phra Rothasen told them that he had to hurry back to live with Meri who was waiting for him.

But meanwhile Meri had died of sorrow. During her long wait she had shed so many tears that she had become blind. Before she died, she solemnly vowed that she would follow Phra Rothasen in every future reincarnation. Then she died with her grandmother crying at her side and surrounded by her servants.

When Phra Rothasen arrived to the ogre kingdom he realized it was too late. He heard about her vow and carried his wife's body. Full of sadness at having lost everything, he dropped dead while holding his wife in his arms. Finally, their spirits flew together to their next rebirth where they would be joined again.

In Tambon Mon Nang, Phanat Nikhom District, Chonburi Province, there is a shrine to the Twelve Sisters with the rock they used as pillow when they wandered in the wilderness and a Carissa carandas tree.

Sa Siliam (สระสี่เหลี่ยม), also in Chonburi Province, is said to be the pond where Phra Rothasen brought his cock to drink water when he ran cockfights to make a living for the twelve sisters while they were banished in the deep dark cave, according to a legend of the area.

Cambodian version

In Cambodia this legend is known as *Puthisen Neang Kong Rei*. The story goes thus:

Once upon a time, there was a rich man who turned to a poor man because of his twelve daughters. So he abandoned his daughters in a deep forest. There the giant Neang Santema took the 12 foundlings to be the servants of her daughter, Kong Rei.

Eventually tiring of the toil of their lives under the terrifying giants, the 12 fled their bondage and made their way to a neighboring kingdom where they were wed en masse to its king, Preah Bath Rothasith.

But the giant Santema was unwilling to allow the dozen former servants of her daughter to live in even the relative freedom that polygamous relationships of the time allowed. Instead, Santema concealed her identity - not a small matter considering her physical stature and reputation - and charmed Rothasith into making her his 13th wife.

Once she had gained the trust and sympathy of her new husband, Santema feigned a deadly illness, one that all the doctors and medicines of her husband failed to cure.

Santema capitalized on Rothasith's growing desperation and informed him that only a potion concocted from the eyeballs of her 12 pregnant co-wives would save her life. Entranced by Santema's wiles, Roth-asith ordered his soldiers to carve out the eyes of 11 of the 12 women, with wife Neang Pov allowed to keep one of her eyes.

After their ritual mutilation, the now blind or nearly blind women were confined in a cave, where they were forced to consume their newly born children one by one.

Only one-eyed Neang Pov was allowed to let her son, Puthisan, survive. In the darkness of the cave with his blind, grief-crazed aunts, Sen quietly fortified himself with dreams of revenge as he nourished himself with the flesh of his dead cousins.

When he became an adult, the evil Santema began to fear the consequences if Puthisan became King. To circumvent any possible acts of revenge by Sen, Santema sent him a letter instructing him to use it for passage into the Forest of Giants. In fact, the letter was a death warrant that stated "When Pothisan arrives, eat him".

But the letter was cunningly altered by a hermit living in the forest to read : "When Puthisan arrives, marry him to my daughter."

Thus when Pothisan entered the Forest of Giants, the letter was read and its instructions obeyed by the sentinel giants. Unbeknownst to Santema, her beloved daughter Kong Rei became the adoring wife of her greatest enemy.

After their married, Kong Rei had told Puthisan all about the magic thing in her Kingdom including the Eyeballs that belonged to Puthisen's mother and aunts. Predictably, rather than fulfilling his conjugal duties Puthisen took advantage of his new position to steal back the eyeballs of his long-suffering aunts along with some magical potions designed to facilitate his escape.

When a stricken Kong Rei attempted to pursue Sen, he used the magical potion to turn the land between them into water, allowing him to flee. Kong Rei cried and begged him to come back to live with her but he refused cause he should thought of his mother stronger than wife. Kong rei cried until she died and became the Mountain called Kong Rei Mountain at Kampong Chhnang

When he arrived in his kingdom, he made his mother and aunts have their eyeballs again and killed Santema. Finally, Putisan, his mother and aunts lived happily in the royal palace with Santema's body turned to stone and abandoned in the deep forest.

Phnom Kong Rei is a mountain in Kampong Chhnang Province, Central Cambodia. The silhouette of the mountain seen from afar looks like a sleeping lady. According to local folklore this mountain is related to the story. Kompong Cham province of Cambodia as the temple of the 12 sisters rest in Siemreap, Cambodia. The story was adapted to movie and released in 1968.

Lao version

The Lao version of the Twelve Sisters, the story of Putthasen (Buddhasen), was translated into French by Louis Finot in 1917.

A merchant fell into poverty and abandoned his twelve daughters in the forest.

Two mountains located close together facing Luang Prabang on the right bank of the Mekong are named Phu Tao Putthasen and Phu Nang Kankari, after Putthasen and Kankari.

Popular culture

Films and soap operas

The story has been adapted to Thai films, Thai television soap operas

(ละคร) and Khmer films.

In Khmer
Puthisen Neang Kong Rey (1972 Film).
Rithisen Neang Kong Rei (2000 film).

In Thai
Phra Rot Meri Ruea Nang Sip Song
Phra Rod Meree (1981 film)
Nang Sib song (1983 Lakorn)
Nang Sib Song (1987 lakorn).
Phra Rodasan (lakorn)
Nang Sib Song (lakorn) (2000).
The Adventure of 12 Ladies Thai animated movie.
Prasuton Manora (2003)

Other media
The Twelve Sisters story has been adapted as well to local printed media, such as books, children's books, Thai comics in classical style and in manga.

The theme of the story of the Twelve Ladies is ever popular and is also found in traditional theatre, dances, poetry and songs.

Source http://en.wikipedia.org/wiki/The_Twelve_Sisters

Vessantara Jataka

Vessantara Jataka mural, 19th century, Wat Suwannaram, Thonburi district, Bangkok, Thailand

Vessantara Jataka mural, Wat Phnom, Phnom Penh, Cambodia. The girl Amittada is beaten up by the village girls, humiliated she goes to complain to her old husband.

The **Vessantara Jataka** (Burmese: ???????? ????????, Wethandaya Zatdaw; Thai: มหาเวสสันดรชาดก, Maha Wetsandon Chadok) is one of the most popular avadānas of Theravada Buddhism. The Vessantara Jataka tells the story of one of Buddha's past lives, about a compassionate prince, Vessantara, who gives away everything he owns, including his children, thereby displaying the virtue of perfect charity. It is also known as the **Great Birth Sermon**.

Description
When Gautama Buddha visited his father's kingdom for the first time after he achieved the supreme enlightenment, arrogant elders of the ruling dynasty did not pay him respect, since they were older than 'Siddhartha Rajakumar'. The Buddha miraculously appeared in the air above his relatives. His father was the first to bow down and admitted that this was his third time to pay respect to his own son. Members of the dynasty then bowed down and accepted the religion. Suddenly, rain clouds gathered and a red-drop rain appeared. This miracle led to his followers' asking, "What is this rain?" He then explained that this rain had appeared once before, during his last life before his present life. Then, he told them the story of his previous life as King Vessantara.

King Vessantara was the son of Sañjaya, king of *Sivirattha* (*Sivi-Rashtra*), and was born in the capital city of *Jatuttara* as a Bodhisattva.

His mother, according to tradition, was a princess who made great merit and wished to become the mother of a future Bodhisattva who would be the next Buddha. After she died, the princess ascended to the Celestial Kingdom and became one of the god Indra's consorts. She lived happily until the day she had to be reborn again as a human. Indra gave her 10 boons and one of them was 'Let me become the mother of Bodhisattva, who in his next life will achieve enlightenment'. She descended to the human world, was born to the court of a king, and later married to King Sañjaya.

On the last day of her pregnancy, the Queen wished to sight-see in the capital city. Her husband granted her that wish. She visited several districts, and the people were delighted by their queen. While she was in the merchant quarter, she gave birth in an emergency delivery at the bazaar, in the heart of the city. Therefore, the newborn prince and heir was named Vessantara, which means 'Born in the merchant quarter'. As soon as he opened his eyes, the infant prince asked his mother for money to give to the poor. On the same day, a female elephant brought her newborn calf to the royal palace. The calf was pure white.

Vessantara grew up to be a kind person who was willing to give away his belongings to others. His parents were delighted by their son's character and supported the prince's charity with their treasures. Vessantara married princess Maddi. They had 2 children: the Prince Jali and the Princess Kanhajina. Sañjaya retired and Vessantara was crowned King.

One day Vessantara gave away the magical white elephant, which had brought rain to his kingdom, to envoys from Kalinga, a neighboring country which was facing a drought. The citizens of Vessantara's kingdom were distressed by the fear of drought because of the loss of the elephant. Thus, they convinced King Sanjaya to resume control of the kingdom and banish his son Vessantara.

The king readily gave away his kingdom to his father. Before leaving the city and going to live in the forest as a hermit with his wife Maddi and their two children, he also gave away his wealth.

One of his loyal courtiers suggested that the family should live at Vamka Mountain. They left the city on a four-horse chariot. Along the way; Vessantara gave away his horses and four deities appeared in the form of stags to pull the chariot. Then he gave away his chariot. The family walked on foot through a forest. The young prince and princess saw wild fruit hanging on high branches, but their parents could not reach it. Miraculously, all the trees bent their branches for them.

The family then arrived at the neighbouring kingdom of Ceti. The king of Ceta was informed of their arrival and rushed to greet the prince. He was touched by their story and offered his throne, but the prince declined. He and his family also declined to stay in a palace. The king of Ceta ordered a hunter to patrol the entrance to Vamka Mountain, to prevent anyone from disturbing the family.

Meanwhile Jujaka, a greedy old Brahmin who lived as a beggar, had a very young wife, Amittada, who was also very beautiful and hard-working. During the drought Amittada used to regularly bring water from the well for her old husband. The husbands of the other women in the village held her up as an example of a good industrious wife. One day, in a fit of jealousy, all the village women gathered by the well and beat up the Brahmin's young wife, tearing her clothes.

In Chapter 11, the children are cared for while Jujaka sleeps. This painting is from the 19th century, Thailand. In the collection of the Walters Art Museum

From that day onwards the girl stubbornly refused to go to the well any longer. Amittada harassed Jujaka telling him to find her some servants in order to spare her more ridicule. She didn't give her husband any peace.

Jujaka met the hunter guarding the entrance to Vamka Mountain and tricked him. He met a rishi and tricked him, as well. Finally, the Brahmin Jujaka went to the forest to prince Vessantara while his wife Maddi was away. He asked him for his two children, which Vessantara readily gave away. Jali and Kanha went to hide in a lotus pond. Their father found them and asked if they would help their father achieve his highest goal. Both agreed and became Jujaka's slaves. Vessantara told the Brahmin to bring his children to their grandfather, saying, "The king will reward you for bringing his beloved grandchildren back to them". Jujaka disagreed, stating the Sunjaya would execute him instead. The Brahmin tied both children with vines and dragged them like cattle. Both children begged their father to help them while the old man scolded and beat them with his stick. Vessantara could not stand this scene and reached for his weapon he kept in his hut. However, he overcame all anger and let his children be taken away.

Maddi's return passage to their resident was blocked by tigers (gods in disguise). When she didn't see her children, she wandered around all night looking for them and finally collapsed before her husband. Vessatara thought she was dead so he lamented his loss. He put her head on his lap and realised that she was still breathing. He revived Maddi with water. She woke up and rose immediately as the couple had taken a vow of celibacy and were not supposed to touch each other. Vessantara told her the what had happened. After Maddi learnt that her husband gave away their children, she praised him for his greatness.

Fearing that Vessantara would have given away his wife as well, God Indra intervened and in disguise, asked for his wife Maddi, which Vessantara readily gave him as well. Then Indra gave Maddi back to Vessantara as a trust, for all his acts of benevolence and generosity had been perfect.

A god and a goddess felt sympathy for the young prince and princess. They disguised themselves as their parents and helped nurse Jali and Kanha. They made Jujaka take a wrong turn and led him to into Sivi Kingdom and through the palace gate. King Sanjaya saw two familiar faces and ordered royal guards to bring them to him. He recognized his grandchildren and paid for their price. Kanha's price was higher than her brother's, as her father wanted no one to buy her from Jujaka. In fact, both Jali and Kanha's prices were so high that only the wealthy king Sanjaya of Sivi could have bought them.

Jujaka became extremely rich. At his first meal as a rich man, he ate too much. His digestive system failed and he fell dead upon his plate. King Sanjaya sent his men to find Jujaka's family to inherit his wealth; however, his wife and in-laws were afraid of the punishment for Jujaka's treason, so they escaped.

Sanjaya arranged a grand procession to meet his son and daughter-in-law. The Kingdom of Kalinga also returned the white elephant, now that Kalinga had become prosperous again, abating the anger of the people of Sivi. Jali led the army and men to his parents' residence and the family was reunited. After the most happy moment, all six of them collapsed.

The red rain poured down from Heaven to revive the family. This rain "soaks those who want to be soaked, but will not fall on those who want to stay dry." Vessantara was crowned as king again and returned to his kingdom. Indra blessed Sivi Kingdom with a seven-gem rain. Vessantara allowed people to keep those gems for themselves and the leftover went into the Kingdom treasury, which he used for his charity. He was also given the blessing of never running out of treasure for his charity.

Lord Buddha explained that each figure had been reborn as people surrounding him. His parents were Vessantara's parents. Maddi was reborn as his former wife. Jali became Rahul, his son. Kanha became Ubolvanna, the Bhikuni (female monk). The loyal courtier who informed him of the place he should stay became Ananda, his cousin and attendant. Jujaka became Devadutt, his arch enemy. The white elephant became Maha Kassapaya.

Festivals and arts

The Vessantara Jataka is celebrated in temples during a Buddhist festival known as *Thet Mahachat* (Thai: เทศน์มหาชาติ), from *Maha Jati* or "Great Birth", in Central Thailand, *Boun Pha Vet* in Laos and as *Bun Phawet* (Bun Phra Wes), *Bun Duan Sii* (Merit-making of the fourth month) or *Thet Phawet* in Isaan. It is also an important celebration as well in Cambodia and Myanmar.

The *Thet Mahachat* is very popular both in rural and urban communities, often with dance and drama performances, as well as festive parades and processions through the towns. During this Buddhist festival the monks give a sermon of all chapters of the Vessantara Jataka, accompanied by rituals and cultural performances. Because of its central role on the *Thet Mahachat* or *Boun Pha Vet* celebrations, the Vessantara Jataka is an important part of the traditional folklore in many areas of the South east Asian region. Some of the scenes, especially the mismatched couple formed by Jujaka, the old Brahmin, and his nagging young wife Amittada, are avidly followed by the average people during the festival. While it has lost its traditional importance in some areas, in others it has gained in popularity.

Scenes of the Vessantara Jataka are engraved on Angkor Wat murals. They are also often found depicted on the walls of Buddhist temples throughout Southeast Asia. This story is also depicted in ancient patterns on matmi silk cloth.

Source http://en.wikipedia.org/wiki/Vessantara_Jataka

Yantra tattooing

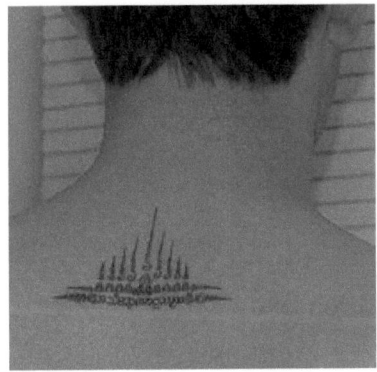

A simple sak yant nine spire (*kau yot*) tattoo

Yantra tattooing, also called **sak yant** (Thai: สักยันต์, Khmer: សាក់យ័ន្ត), is a form of tattooing practiced in Southeast Asian countries including Cambodia, Laos, and Thailand. The practice has also begun to grow in popularity among Chinese Buddhists in Singapore. *Sak* means "to tap [tattoo]", and *yant* is Thai for the Sanskrit word yantra.

Sak yant designs are normally tattooed by *wicha* (magic) practitioners and Buddhist monks, traditionally with a long bamboo stick sharpened to a point (called a *mai sak*) or alternatively with a long metal spike (called a *khem sak*).

History

Origin belongs to Cambodians, with ancient Khmer script writting. During Khmer empire all Khmer Warriors were covered up with tattoo from head to toes. including chest, arms even fingers. King Jayavarman VII, test out with his owned body, being strike by arrows, all hits bounce off his chest. Prove was written in Zhou Daguan dairy. Chinese chronicles describe yantra tattooing among the Thai cultures of southwestern China and northwestern Vietnam at least 2000 years ago. Over the centuries the tradition spread to what is now Thailand, Laos, Cambodia and parts of Myanmar. Today it is most popular in Thailand, whereas in Cambodia and Laos the tradition has almost completely vanished.

The script used for yantra designs varies according to cultural and geographic factors. In Cambodia and central Thailand, Khmer script is used, while in northern Thailand one sees yantra tattoos bearing Shan, Northern Thai or Tai Lu scripts, and in Laos the Lao Tham script is employed. The script spells out abbreviated syllables from Pali incantations. Different masters have added to these designs over the centuries through visions received in their meditations. Some yantra designs have been adapted from pre-Buddhist Shamanism and the belief in animal spirits that was found in the Southeast Asian sub-continent and incorporated into the Thai tradition and cultures.

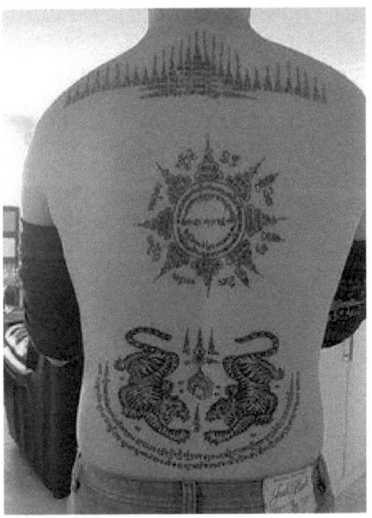

Meaning

Yantra tattoos are believed to be magic and bestow mystical powers, protection, or good luck.

In Cambodia, the tattoo is used for self-protection. Cambodians believe a yantra has magical powers that ward off evil and hardship. The tattoo is particularly popular amongst military personnel. The tattoo supposedly guarantees that the person cannot receive any physical harm as long as they observe certain rules.

Yant designs are also applied to many other media, such as cloth or metal, and placed in one's house, place of worship, or vehicle as a means of protection from danger or illness, increasing wealth, or attracting lovers.

Types and Designs

There are many traditional types and designs of Yantra Tattoos, but some of the most well-known and popular include:

Ongk Phra (Thai: องค์พระ translation: *Buddha's body*) - one of the most commonly used elements in Yantra tattooing but can also be a more complex standalone design. Meant to provide insight, guidance, illumination, etc.

Ha Thaew (Thai: ห้าแถว translation: *five rows*) - one of the most common Yantra designs for women in Thailand but also used for men. Typically tattooed on the back left shoulder. Each of the five lines relates to a different blessing for success and good luck.

Kao Yord (Thai: เก้ายอด translation: *nine spires*) - typically tattooed on the center top of the back in various sizes and levels of complexity. Simple version pictured at the top of this article.

Sii Yord (Thai: สี่ยอด translation: *four spires*) - to influence the feelings or actions of others and protect the bearer.

Paed Tidt (Thai: แปดทิศ translation: *eight points*) - represents protection in the eight directions of the universe. Round shape; typically tattooed on the center of the back. Pictured in gallery below.

Sip Tidt Thai: สิบทิศ(translation: *ten points*) - a version of *Paed Tidt* but protects in ten directions instead of eight.

Mahaniyom (Thai: มหานิยม (translation: *great preference*) - to grant the bearer favor in the eyes of others. Round shape; typically placed on the back right shoulder.

Yord Mongkut (Thai: ยอดมงกุฎ translation: *spired crown*) - for good fortune and protection in battle. Round shape; typically tattooed on the top of the head.

Bpanjamukhee (translation: *five Deva faces*) - intended to ward off illness and danger.

Suea (Thai: เสือ translation: *tiger*) - typically depicts twin tigers. Represents power and authority.

Locations

Many internet sites recommend Thailand as the right place to attain the most refined ritual tattoos and consider the country as the best place for learning this art. Every year, hundreds of foreigners in search of original and magical tattoos come to Thailand to have a Sak Yant. In Southeast Asia, Thailand is by far the country with the highest number of devotees. Sak yant is performed throughout the country in temples in Bangkok, Ayutthaya, and northern Thailand.

One of the most famous temples in the present day for yantra tattooing is Wat Bang Phra in Nakhon Chaysri, Nakhon Pathom Province, Thailand. The power of sacred tattoos decreases with time. So, to re-empower them each year, Sak Yant masters celebrate with their devotees the Wai Khru ritual. Wai Khru, meaning pay homage to one's teacher. In Thailand, the most impressive Wai Khru is held at the temple of Wat Bang Phra.

Ajarn Noo Kanpai, perhaps the most famous practitioner of sak yant in Thailand, trained here.

One well-known temple in northern Thailand is Wat Keam, which means "needle". It is located in San Patong just outside Chiang Mai and home to the sak yant master Phra Ajarn Gamtawn, who died in Chiang Mai on 14 September 2010.

In the Lum Phli area on the north side of Ayutthaya, Thailand, Ajarn Kob and his son, Ajarn Oh, are well-known sak yant masters.

Gallery

Yant Paed Tidt

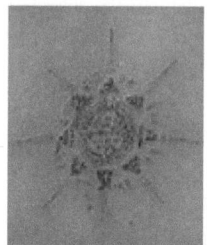

Hlwong Pi Nan tattooing Yant at Wat Bang Phra Temple

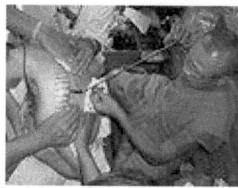

Hlwong Pi Pant tattooing a Yant in Ang Thong Province.

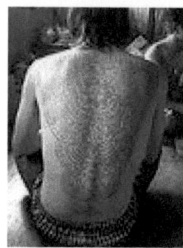

Devotee of Wat Bang Phra covered in Yant Tattoos

sak yant nakhon pathom
Source http://en.wikipedia.org/wiki/Yantra_tattooing